UNCONVENTIONAL

WAYS TO THRIVE IN EDU

RACHELLE DENE POTH

Published by EduMatch®
PO Box 150324, Alexandria, VA 22315
www.edumatchpublishing.com

These books are available at special discounts when purchased in quantities of 10 or more for use as premiums, promotions fundraising, and educational use. For inquiries and details, contact the publisher: sarah@edumatch.org.

ISBN: 978-1-970133-48-6

CONTENTS

by creating waves of unconventional and innovative methods. Together we can effect widespread change and transform the look of learning.

The book will provide educators with ideas to promote creativity, student voice, curiosity for learning, and student agency, while also offering encouragement to do more and to not be afraid to push the limits when it comes to teaching. It will show educators that big changes are possible, sometimes through the slightest shifts. The book and stories will inspire educators to dare to be different!

*** Each chapter starts with a story, whether a movie or tv show reference or a personal narrative to frame the chapter theme. Each chapter ends with takeaways, a reflection, and an encouragement to share and connect on social media.

Believe in yourself and all that you are. Know that there is something inside you that is greater than any obstacle.

CHRISTIAN D. LARSON

BOOK OVERVIEW

My hope for this book is to inspire educators to make some changes in the way we think about teaching practices, methods, activities, roles — anything involving instruction that has been or become the accepted standards or the "norm." We need to move away from what may be considered conventional or traditional methods of teaching, practices which we experienced as students, and may continue in our own classrooms. Starting with one change at a time and doing things in a different, out of the ordinary way and out of one's comfort zone. By taking commonly-held practices and shifting them into an alternate format, that will push back against "the way it has always been done," yet in a way that empowers teachers to take risks. For some, this may feel unconventional, or uncomfortable at times, but the ideas are meant to enhance the types of learning experiences we provide for our students. For me, being unconventional means placing students in the lead more, exploring different and emerging technologies, and having a plan to not have a plan.

I hope that this book will provide ideas and inspiration for educators to take more risks in their practice and bring amazing changes into every classroom every day. To best prepare for the future, we can start

DEDICATION

I am so thankful for the support of my parents, David, and my amazing 53s. I honestly don't know where I would be without this tremendous support. The countless hours spent over the past year, working on multiple projects, facing challenges, experiencing some defeats, but not losing hope and not backing down because of my amazing supportive family.

Thank you, Sarah Thomas, for creating a space for educators to learn, grow, and thrive together. I appreciate you more than you know.

FOREWORD

In the summer of 2015, I had been looking up math proficiency scores for schools all around our state when I was confronted with some data that I never expected. (We were competitive with our test scores, and I wanted to know where we ranked, relative to other schools around the state.) For most grades, the same predictable schools led the way, and the top few spots were always dominated by the usual high achievers. These were schools in affluent school districts whose students had every advantage imaginable when taking standardized tests. But that year, I noticed there was a small, somewhat obscure school, whose fourth-grade math scores were tied for number one in the entire state. And this school had almost forty percent of their student population served by free or reduced lunch. This was an anomaly that piqued my attention!

In a small school, the test scores can often rest on the shoulders of just one or two teachers in each grade. I had to find out who this fourth-grade math teacher was. This teacher wasn't just beating the odds; she was destroying them. So that summer, I sent an email to the principal. I introduced myself; I congratulated him on the academic achievements of his students (especially his fourth-grade math students!), and

I asked if I could come for a visit. The principal responded graciously and welcomed a visit. So, I took a two-hour road trip to uncover the "magic" behind these phenomenal results. I remember sitting in the principal's office and asking him what was going on in fourth-grade math. He said, "I've got two teachers. One of them is really good, and the other one is off the charts amazing." So, I asked him, "Tell me about the one who is off the charts amazing. What makes her so awesome?" He paused, was quiet, and didn't seem to have a response. He seemed to be caught off guard by my question, almost as if he hadn't really considered the qualities that defined his teacher. Finally, he said: "She's just relentless. She'll do anything to help a student understand math. She'll try any strategy. She'll find any resource. She'll do whatever it takes for her students to be successful." That was it.

It wasn't about the right program. It wasn't about the newest technology. And there was no magic. It was a teacher who defined her success by the success of her students. It was a teacher who was willing to do whatever it took for her students to learn -- for her students to thrive. That was several years ago… but I'm still inspired thinking about that teacher.

That is the sort of teacher who has written this book. Rachelle Dene Poth is a teacher who models an extraordinary commitment to the students in her classroom, and whose passion for education extends beyond the walls of a classroom or even a school building. She knows the challenges that confront teachers, but she is keenly aware of the potential that has yet to be tapped in classrooms across the country. Rachelle finds joy in the classroom, but she also finds joy in the profession. She is on a mission to connect teachers, to inspire teachers, and to empower teachers.

Unconventional is for every educator who is looking to take it to the next level. You've picked up the book… which means it was written for you. You're the teacher who is good at your job, but you know you could be better. You're the teacher who connects with your students, but you know those relationships could be stronger. You're the teacher who has started to push the professional envelope, but you know you could push it further.

There are many amazing teachers, but none of them started out that way. They became amazing because they made lots of little decisions to rise above mediocrity. They refused to settle for average. As teachers grow in their profession, their content knowledge increases; their collection of resources increases; their repertoire of instructional strategies expands, and their overall job satisfaction is enhanced. As educators, they are *thriving*. But ultimately, the goal is never about the enhanced job satisfaction of educators. The goal is to make a difference for students! *Thriving* teachers make it possible for our classrooms to be full of *thriving students*! When teachers start reaching their potential as educators, it opens the door for students to start reaching their potential as learners. And Rachelle gets it.

Remember that fourth-grade math teacher who was "off the charts amazing?" She didn't have a special degree; she had a special mindset. As educators, we don't become amazing by playing it safe all the time. If you want to be awesome, you have to take some risks. You have to be willing to reevaluate the status quo. This book is for you. It is full of ideas, full of poignant stories, and full of inspiration. The students of Rachelle Dene Poth are lucky to have her as their teacher -- as your students are lucky to have you. It has been said that "excellence is a journey, not a destination." We will never "arrive" at that destination -- but as educators, we continue to push on because the stakes are high. Our students deserve our best. This book is part of your journey. Thanks for picking it up.

Danny Steele

Educator, Author, and Speaker

UNCONVENTIONAL

I don't really want to become normal, average, standard. I want merely to gain in strength, in the courage to live out my life more fully, enjoy more, experience more. I want to develop even more original and more unconventional traits.

ANAIS NIN, ESSAYIST

INTRODUCTION

As an only child, many of my days were focused on school. For me, school was an opportunity to be social. It was fun because I could be with my friends and I enjoyed being around my teachers. There was always so much to do to pass the time. Different activities, opportunities to learn new words, worksheets, color, read books, all things that I loved to do. When I wasn't in school, I was at home playing school.

Because my parents worked and did not get home most evenings until around 6:30, my grandparents would usually pick me up and stay with me until my parents got home. My grandma and I played school on many of those days. Of course, I would be the teacher, and my grandma would be my student. I would ask her questions, typically about things I had learned that day. I was excited that I was teaching her new things, or so I thought. I knew that she had not been a student in many years, and her days were spent working on the farm, cooking, or doing things around the house. While I loved sharing what I was learning with her, there were times that I wanted her to be the teacher and ask me questions. I wanted to show what I had learned, maybe even show off a little, but I wanted her to be proud of me. She always went along with what I wanted and often had me reciting times tables, spelling words, practicing mnemonic devices for remembering the Great Lakes, or naming state capitals. I would give her my lists, tests, worksheets to use to ask me questions.

I still have all of those facts committed to memory to this day, around 40 years later, because of our relationship. She was supportive, and she always encouraged me along the way. My time with her was always so special. I was often sad when the school day ended, but excited to go home and find my grandma waiting for me because we always had fun learning. Although I did not realize until reflecting back and writing, I was teaching her too.

Once my parents came home, we would spend time working on my homework. My mom or dad would quiz me, and then I was off to bed to repeat the same routine the next day. So, looking back, most of my time was spent going to school in some form. With so much time studying and playing school, you would think that I probably had straight A's, or close to it. While I did well in most of my classes, of course, there were some that I struggled in, like math and reading comprehension. For the most part, my elementary school experience was positive. I felt supported and comfortable and enjoyed the teachers that I had.

In my small elementary school, some teachers showed you that you mattered more than the content. These teachers were always in their classrooms, ready to greet you, with everything set up for class, and they welcomed you in with a smile and conversation. These teachers stopped what they were doing and gave you their full attention, speaking with kind words, and letting you know that it was okay to make mistakes and to be *different*. And I was different.

Knowing just the right words to say to encourage you to keep trying. But not all teachers were like that, and I had some experiences that left me feeling like I didn't belong, that I wasn't smart enough, and that I wasn't good enough. The reason I am sharing this is because although I remember the way these teachers made me feel, it has served as a reminder of the importance of how we treat others and letting others know that they matter. Especially as teachers, we interact with so many people every single day and as brief as these interactions may be, they all mean *something*. We can never fully know the impact of our words, our actions, and our responses that students pick up on. So, it starts with us to build a solid foundation for all students to learn and connect in our space. We are in a position to impact not only those in our classrooms and schools, but every person who our students connect with in the future.

I've had many supportive and inspirational "teachers." My first teachers were my parents and grandparents, who taught me the value of education, the importance of working hard, and persistence. My parents provided the support that I needed and inspired me to keep on learning. I have also been fortunate to have one teacher who made such an impact on me that it led me to redefine who I needed to be(come) as an educator. Bruce Antkowiak, not only a law school professor, but more importantly, a mentor, friend, and role model, who completely transformed my confidence in myself as a student. He was a professor who not only shared who he was and what he stood for, but also taught us that we all need to share our story. I am grateful to him for inspiring me to do more in my own classroom and changing my beliefs about what it means to be an educator today.

I have always been a rather private person, especially when it comes to my teacher persona. As someone who does not have children of her own, making a change to how I connect with students has impacted me tremendously. With a new perspective on student-teacher relationships, I have shared more of who I am, what I do, and what I believe in. I have laughed more and let go some. By opening myself up more to connecting with students, I have noticed a big difference in my classroom and for me personally and professionally. Being able to share the love of a certain movie or a book or even just having a favorite food in common goes a long way toward building a connection with that one student who needs you the most. The students need to know us as much as we need to know them. Relationships matter.

"Above all else, be daring, be bold, be unconventional."

KEVIN RAMPE

Above all else, be DARING, be BOLD, be UNCONVENTIONAL.

—Kevin Rampe

H. LIPPERT

1 RELATIONSHIPS ARE THE FOUNDATION

"It's the little conversations that build the relationships and make an impact on each student."

ROBERT JOHN MEEHAN, AMERICAN POET

Who You Are

Have you seen the movie *Stand and Deliver?* It is a 1988 movie based on the life of Jaime Escalante (portrayed by Edward James Olmos), a high school teacher from Los Angeles. In the movie, Escalante is hired to teach computer science, but due to a lack of funding, he is reassigned to teaching a remedial math class. Jaime is placed in a classroom with students of mixed behaviors and abilities, and who are considered to be disruptive and incapable of learning. He recognizes that the students are capable of doing more, so he pushes them to learn more than regular math, and instead decides to teach them calculus. Throughout the movie, you see Jaime's struggles, and what he does to overcome the challenges and to push back against those who don't believe in the students' abilities. He pushes back even when it is the students who doubt themselves, to show them that they can do it.

At first, his students do not really like him and likely do not trust him, as their personal lives represent a conflict between family and school and the choices that they each have to make. Yet he continues to alter his manner of teaching to meet their needs and interests. He encourages students to have "ganas," the motivation and desire to succeed. To connect with them, he goes beyond the classroom and learns about each student. He provides more than just instruction. He gives of himself to lift them up, to help when needed, and does not give up on them, nor does he let them give up on themselves. He goes into their world. He goes to a restaurant where a young student works to talk to her family about her future. He wants to better understand the challenges they each face. He builds upon this to do more than just teach them about calculus; he teaches them about life.

Even though there is a high incidence of dropout in the school and others expect the students to fail, Jaime persists in helping them to learn calculus and ultimately to pass the AP Calculus Exam. The students all pass, but their scores are questioned, and they have to take the test again to prove that they did not cheat. In spite of what seems like defeat, together they face the test again and prove they had what it took to pass when they had the belief of a teacher. This story emphasizes the importance of relationships and what it sometimes takes to make those connections with students—a teacher who used unconventional methods to make a difference in the lives of students in an unconventional class.

"The strength of our student relationships makes the difference in translating our passion for teaching into their passion for learning."

BETH MORROW, STRATEGIC CONSULTANT, TEACHER

For most of my first fifteen years of teaching, I believed that I had to start each new school year by explaining course expectations, providing a class syllabus, and sending forms home for parents to sign, all on the first day. It was how I had been taught, and it became the most comfortable for *me*. Thinking about this today makes me cringe. There was the belief, *my* belief, that teachers needed to maintain a certain presence in the classroom and that a clearly-defined student-teacher relationship existed. Teachers taught, enforced rules, and followed lesson plans. Being a teacher meant that you didn't go too far beyond delivering the content, assessing students, and making sure that the rules were followed. For some teachers, smiling or having fun in class was not considered to be appropriate. Often heard advice was to not smile before the holiday break. For many years, I didn't.

From personal experience as a student and during my teacher education program, this is what the student-teacher relationships looked like. At most, it was okay to share educational background, minor personal facts like food preferences, or maybe favorite music—general topics that might come up in class discussions (although at times, I thought that this might be too much to share). My perception was that the time in the classroom was for learning, only talking about the content, and working toward the set learning goals. However, I started to see the student-teacher relationship a bit differently about ten years into my teaching career.

My experience with my law school professor Bruce Antkowiak taught me that relationships must come first, before everything else, and they do not end when the class does. No matter how hectic a teacher's schedule might become, we must stop, lean in, and listen whenever a student needs us. Student needs come first. We show this by being present, greeting students at the door, and welcoming them in each day. When teachers take time to talk to students about their day or attend their events, conversations will become more commonplace, the connections will start to form and continue to grow. Students will know that they are cared for, feel more comfortable, and develop more confidence. This is what we want for our students.

Dr. James Comer stated, "No significant learning occurs without a relationship." While there are many interpretations of this quote and what Dr. Comer meant, I have kept this quote in my mind. I strongly believe that it is through the building and fostering of relationships that we can create better possibilities for learning and facilitate a welcoming environment where student-driven learning is possible. If we want our students to thrive, there are two areas we need to be mindful of as educators: relationships and reflections. We need to start every new school year, each day, and after each interaction with our students, trying to make a difference in the lives of our students.

In her famous TED talk, the late Rita Pierson said, "Every child needs a champion—a person who will not give up on students." This is a powerful message emphasizing the importance of knowing our students, a message that has served as my daily reminder to always make time for students, no matter what. We must take time to connect and fully invest in not just what we are doing in our role as the "teacher," but more importantly, why we have chosen to be in education. We also need to reflect on our methods and our interactions, asking ourselves whether we are doing enough, what could we do better, and how can we improve tomorrow. To create the best opportunities for students to learn and grow and be successful, we must be unconventional in building rapport and developing these relationships in our classrooms.

Building Relationships Requires an Everyday Commitment

There are no quick tricks or ways to build relationships. It is not something that can be done in one day, nor can it truly be accomplished over a short time. We want to create long-lasting connections that will be(come) vital to the growth and success of the students in our classrooms as well as ourselves. Think back to your own experiences as a student.

- In which classes did you feel the most supported, and how did it impact your performance?
- Now, compare two teachers/classes: one where you felt supported and valued as a learner, and another where perhaps you felt unsupported or even had a negative experience. What was the impact, if any, on your ability to learn in these courses? How much do you remember about the content covered if your classroom experience was negative?

When I was younger, there were some classes that I could tell the teacher only cared about covering the lesson, assigning and collecting homework, and nothing more. It was hard to connect. I had my own negative experiences and remember very little if any of the content. I remember how I felt in those classes, and it hurt my confidence in succeeding.

Choosing Our Words Carefully: The Impact of Words on
Relationships

Some of the greatest lessons I learned about being a teacher came
from thinking about my own negative experiences as a student in the
seventh and ninth grade. It is not always the words that teachers say.
It can be the feedback they give, or simply a gesture that might seem
like nothing at all, but that can have a negative effect on student
achievement or confidence. As a child who doubted her own ability
and lacked confidence, I needed for my teachers to support and
encourage me.

Algebra was a struggle for me in the seventh grade. It was the first
time that I was not earning As or Bs and instead took home Cs and
mostly Ds. Most evenings, my dad would help me with my algebra
homework, buying books with sample problems, so we could work
through them together. I asked for help in class, but not many of my
questions were answered. I was told to "figure it out" and "try again."
While I understand that we want students to experience some
productive struggle in learning, I know as a seventh-grader then, and
as a teacher now, we need to support students along the way. I recall
one interaction that left me feeling defeated, embarrassed, and
anxious to get out of the room. This interaction reminds me to be a
source of encouragement and a mentor for all students and to always
pause before speaking. Even the slightest interactions matter.

I don't remember if it happened often, and I may have forgotten or
just let it go because who was I to say anything about a teacher? I
remember having an early dismissal one day, and when I raised my
hand to be excused, my teacher said, "What do you want?" I
responded, "I have an early dismissal." There was a brief silence, and
then my teacher rolled her eyes, threw her arms in the air, and with an
irritated-sounding voice, said, "Well, go ahead then."

As a twelve-year-old, this made me feel awkward and embarrassed as
all of my classmates were looking at me and laughing. I know that my

embarrassment showed, and I'm sure I wanted to cry. My teacher noticed my reaction, and when I started to leave, I heard her say, "Rachelle, don't go away mad, just go away." And then she laughed and so did my classmates. I remember getting into my grandmother's car and crying on the way home. I was hurt. I didn't want to go back to school the next day. Why would I? I was made fun of in front of my entire class, by my teacher, and in a class in which I was not doing well to begin with. It stopped me from feeling like I could ask for help. It felt like I didn't matter. I kept it to myself and hoped that she would just leave me alone for the rest of the year.

Nothing was ever said about that interaction. I never even told my parents, but it really bothered me, and still does today, although for different reasons. I cannot imagine speaking to a student in that manner. Those words had a negative impact on a student looking for support from teachers, but instead finds ridicule. It is stamped in my mind, but it has been a motivation for me as a teacher. Even in negative experiences, there are always lessons to be learned. Lessons which can help us to do better by sharing our stories to help others be better too.

There was one other time a hurtful comment made in front of my classmates had an impact on my confidence. It was as a ninth-grader in art class. I have never been, nor will I ever be good at drawing, but it wasn't for lack of trying. I was excited to take art and couldn't wait to start my own projects like the ones that I had seen on display in the school. I mistakenly thought that I could create the same beautiful artwork. Our first assignment was to draw an animal and paint it different shades of one color. I drew a bear and chose brown. It wasn't the best thing I've ever drawn, but I was impressed with how well I had done. My happiness was short-lived because my teacher came over and looked at it, gave half a smile, and said, "I guess this is okay, but I don't think you're going to do too well in this class," on day three of a 180-day school year. Right in front of my classmates. Where's the hope for succeeding or the motivation to try? (As a side note, I still have the drawing, with the grade, and a comment, in red ink).

What a teacher
doesn't say .
. . is a telling
part of what
a student hears.

~ Maurice Natanson

These two experiences teach a valuable lesson: always be mindful of our words, our actions, and even our gestures/body language. Students need our support, and for some, having the confidence to speak up or feel comfortable in class might be a real challenge. We are in a powerful position to make a positive impact on our students. We need to make them feel special so they know that they matter. Giving our students anything less than that is not acceptable.

MAYBE YOUR OWN negative experiences have made you more cognizant of interactions with students and how quickly words can impact them. Our facial expressions and gestures can convey an unintended message to students. We have to be mindful of the message we're sending, especially when we do not intend to send one. The lesson from these two experiences is that words leave a lasting mark on students, greater than we might realize. In a space where they may already feel left out or lacking in confidence, they need to feel supported. The one person they need to be able to count on is the teacher. And if we are the ones who are knocking them down, what's going to happen then? Who will be there to lift them up?

Be Intentional

Relationship-building must be a critical part of planning for every day. Curriculum is important, and our purpose as educators should be to create diverse and authentic learning experiences for students—learning experiences that are full of choices so students can achieve success and leave our classrooms prepared for whatever the future may bring. While we cannot predict the paths they will take, we know that students need to be able to collaborate, communicate, and find a supportive peer network. Even more important, when students leave our classrooms, they need to know that they can always come back to us for our support.

"Everyone who remembers his own education remembers teachers, not methods and techniques. The teacher is the heart of the educational system."

SIDNEY HOOK, AMERICAN PHILOSOPHER

Relationships First, Relationships Always

As educators, one of our most important daily responsibilities is the development of relationships and building rapport with students. Our goal is to create a connection with students and to develop the trust that needs to exist between teachers and students in our classrooms. In doing this, we expand the traditional role of classroom teacher, by shifting toward the provision of a trustworthy, supportive mentorship for students.

Everyone wants to feel welcome, and when we create opportunities for students to connect to their peers, we guide them toward developing crucial social-emotional skills to be successful in college, career, and life. An important part of our work is helping students to develop the life skills they need to be successful and be prepared to face challenges, make decisions, and work as part of a team. When students have that connection, they feel safe, supported, and valued. Beyond simply learning the content, we need to focus on relationship building, to help students begin building their own personal learning networks (PLN). Having the support of a PLN when facing challenges is vital to our growth as educators. Our students need to have the same systems, and by encouraging them to build their own networks, they will emerge as connected learners.

How can these connections be fostered? Where do we find the time needed to build these connections, especially when the traditional classroom teaching structure and activities have focused more on planning instruction, grading, and clerical tasks?

With all of these responsibilities, there is not enough time, if any at all, for students to interact. To show more of who we are and what we are bringing into the classroom, we need to include activities that enable teachers and students, all learners in the classroom, to interact more through authentic and meaningful conversations with one another. We need to shift from the conventional relationship of teacher as leader, and involve students more in the daily work we do. We must also be co-learners, together finding new ways to take risks with learning. Doing this requires a change in practice and procedure, and a willingness to boldly step out of our comfort zones.

We Are in This Together

Deciding how to do this at first can feel uncomfortable because many teachers might view a distinct line of separation between the students and themselves. There is a "line" that separates what should and should not be talked about and shared, and perhaps a focus on only covering the content and nothing more. However, in order to really provide meaningful learning experiences for our students, we need to find a connection point between us and be flexible enough in our lessons to allow for pop-up conversations that may divert us from the lesson. When we find a commonality, it goes back to those relationships and how critical it is that we form them in our classroom.

Showing students that we care and likely have many things in common with one another, as well as differences, will benefit us all through the collaborative relationship that results. Students will feel valued, and teachers will better understand students' needs. It will start us on a path to success for building our classroom culture and creating a welcoming learning space for everyone. We can then see, know, and understand who our students are. And our students can see, know, and understand who we are too.

As we work toward building relationships, the stronger our students will become, the higher the learning potential will be. When we strive to understand our students, where they come from, and figuring out who they are, we allow ourselves to make connections, and students will know that they matter. As the quote by Teddy Roosevelt says, "Nobody cares how much you know until they know how much you care." Let's start by letting ourselves really be seen and open the doors to communication.

A good teacher must be able
to put himself in the place of
those who find learning hard.
 ⁻ Eliphas Levi, French Author

@fishrich

Show Them You Care

How can we best provide for our students? Are there some methods, tools, and resources that work better than others? I can think of one. Relationships. We need to think about how we can build relationships and how it helps us to engage students more in learning. It does not require much; even quick interactions can make a big difference. While we may never know the impact of our short interactions and what it meant to a particular student, the best that we can do is to make sure we are visible and welcome all students into our classrooms. We need to promote peer collaboration and focus on fostering those relationships in the classroom. Sometimes it's as simple as a smile to acknowledge a student that can make a world of difference in their day.

A Plan to Know One Another

"Sometimes a simple, almost insignificant gesture on the part of a teacher can have a profound formative effect on the life of a student."

PAULO FREIRE, BRAZILIAN EDUCATOR

The slightest interactions can do so much. We must be present, which means more than just greeting students at the door. We must make time to listen and to engage students in conversations, and even just a smile lifts them and us up. Positivity goes a long way. We can learn so much through quick conversations with students as they enter the room or by including fun activities in our lesson. Our classrooms should be welcoming spaces where students feel valued. When students feel valued, they know that they matter, they are part of the decisions in our classroom, and they know we will make time for them when they need it. Engaging in some of these practices will help to build and foster positive relationships and connect us with our students.

An unconventional teacher can start by getting out of the way and instead make room for students to take the lead. The beginning of the school year is the perfect time to start building connections; however, any day is an opportunity to start fresh. Each day brings new opportunities to continue learning and growing together. It's okay to laugh and have fun and to cast the lesson aside to make time for authentic interactions. We have to be flexible with our practice and recognize that sometimes, learning happens in different, spontaneous, and wonderful ways.

If the classroom space has students sitting in rows of desks and passively learning rather than actively engaging in the content, we are providing even fewer opportunities for students to build peer collaboration skills or experience a positive classroom culture. It makes it more difficult for us to get to know them. Students need to connect with one another and with the teacher. The unconventional teacher knows that sometimes big changes are needed, and even some which may seem to cause chaos and be uncomfortable. But this creative chaos will lead to innovative, fun learning opportunities. Be ready to dive in!

Creating Our Learning Spaces

Start by taking one day to focus on your classroom. Look around closely at the space: the walls and where the students sit and process the interactions you have with them before, during, and after class. Do the following:

1. Ask yourself, "Does this space work for *them or for me?*" If it's more about you, it is time to make some changes. Like what? Have students display their work, design the set-up of the room, choose the art and decorations for their learning space.

2. Think about your teaching methods and look closely at the setup of your classroom. Some questions you might consider are:

- Who is doing most of the talking?
- What are the students doing during class?
- Where are you located in the room? If you have been the one doing most of the talking, from the front center of the room, then it's time to adjust. How much can you expect to connect with each student by staying in the front of the room?

3. Think about how you interact with your students. Are you truly building relationships with them? Are students able to interact and learn about one another? If not, then perhaps start as I did, by creating different spaces where students have an opportunity to more actively learn, to create and lead, and to do more than just simply sit and take in information. Ask students what they want to learn for the day; it may be unconventional, but involving students will lead to bigger opportunities for learning.

4. Provide opportunities for collaborative work by structuring lessons and creating activities that promote student interaction and the development of "soft skills." Setting aside time for students to work on the content together, even encouraging them to come up with their own ways to practice will not only amplify their learning potential, but will help them develop their interpersonal skills and self-awareness.

THESE SOMEWHAT UNCONVENTIONAL but intentional strategies will help us to better understand and connect with our students. We will positively impact the learning environment by providing the necessary social-emotional learning support our students need. What is better than being able to sit and learn with and from your students?

Venturing into New Territory

Change was needed. For so long in my classroom, there was structure, consistency, and not enough to truly engage students. I had engagement all wrong. Spontaneity takes over. One day, the desks are scattered into groups before the bell rings. A teacher hurries to greet students at the door, and avoids planting in the front and talking *at* the students. Minutes go by in the period, there is confusion, there are questions, and it is a little chaotic. But there has been a transformation. Breaking apart the rows, a first step in bringing about positive change for students and fostering a supportive peer network. While the change at first was a bit unnerving, because this is not what traditional teaching and learning should look like, this unconventional and spontaneous change brought with it positive transformations for learning. My classroom became a better learning space.

Mixing It Up

Sometimes you need to mix things up and take a chance with some icebreakers in the classroom. If you have never done this before, it might feel like a bit of a risk because not everyone is a fan of these activities. How many times have you had to participate in an activity, mix with other groups, or join another group after you already settled into your own perfectly comfortable space with people you know? We need to help our students interact and feel comfortable together. Why not try some icebreakers to get them and you moving around more and connecting?

Start by thinking about each group of students to determine which type of icebreaker activity might work best. By starting small with some basic icebreakers, and joining in with them, it can be easier to build comfort for students to work with their peers in small groups.

Quick Ideas

1) Truths and a Lie

We can't truly understand other people solely based on appearance or after very brief interactions with them. There are a few quick ways to get started, and some simply require paper or digital tools. Sometimes it's fun at the beginning of the year to have students engage in an activity of "truths and a lie." Whether you use 2 or 3 truths does not matter; the idea is to get to know one another. Students can use paper and list their facts or simply share them in front of the class, kind of an improv. But we have to be mindful of student comfort if early in the school year, especially if students have recently moved into the school or transitioned from a different school building. It is vital to support students as they become more comfortable in speaking in the classroom. An idea to help students with this is to use a digital tool like Buncee. Buncee has templates for 3 truths and a lie, and other options for students to create and then share with classmates. These options provide possibilities for all students to explore and find something unique to them.

2) About Me and DNA

There are digital tools with different templates that students can use to show creativity, although this is not an activity that relies on technology. Students can create an "About Me" drawing or graphic and respond to five or six prompts to share with classmates. Based on the responses, have students get into small groups to discuss, share ideas and experiences to continue working on those peer relationships. Another great idea learned from friends on Twitter (Heather Lippert & Laurie McIntosh) is the "DNA" (Dreams, Needs, and Abilities) Activity. Students who may not necessarily feel like drawing or using technology can simply create a "DNA" card on which they list responses to these three themes. The DNA card can be used as a quick 1:1 interview and posted in the room. What a unique way to see that others have similar dreams, needs, and abilities! This is a more unconventional way to get students talking, rather than trying to force conversations.

All three images courtesy of Amy DeFriese

3) Sketchnoting

At the start of the year, after sensing some negativity about school from the students, I held an impromptu discussion and asked them to share some of their frustrations. Most revolved around what they called "repetitive learning activities." One of the main frustrations was that the students thought they did way too much writing in their classes. Constantly taking notes, filling in packets, writing reports, coming up with long answers to questions, and filling in outlines. It was not that students did not want to learn, they just wished they had different options for learning. One thing I have noticed is that students doodle a lot. I see it a lot while I am teaching. The verbs are conjugated in creative charts, with stylish fonts and arrows to emphasize key facts, and drawings represent vocabulary. I took it as an opportunity to teach about sketchnotes and created an activity for them to try sketchnoting out called "This is Me." My goal was to help students learn about sketchnoting and have a more visual way to engage with the content.

How it Works

Students each receive an index card, and on it, they write their name, single words, or images to represent themselves (who they are and what they are about). The idea is that if they were to hold the card up or post it online, it gives a snapshot of the student. Of course, as with all things, there may be a little pushback. Students who don't feel very creative or don't think they have artistic skills may struggle with thinking about what to draw. To get them started, try sharing some drawings of your own, especially if you are like me and do not excel in drawing, making that connection helps to create a sense of comfort with all students. As a side note, this was the first time in my years of teaching that I drew for my students. What stopped me before? Memories of my ninth-grade art class.

Work Together, Learn Together

As teachers, what we should do is participate in the activities that we ask our students to do. It creates a more meaningful experience. By joining in, we show that there is always something to learn and that we are willing to step out of our comfort zone. As someone who doubts her creative and artistic abilities, I started by sharing two of my own sketchnotes, one in its beginning stages and one mostly completed, to show students that it's not about the ability to draw. It's about representing yourself or something with a mixture of text and images. It's about doing something different and not worrying about it being perfect. It was a risk for the first time, but seemed to work well, especially for those students who enjoy doodling and definitely for visual learners. An added bonus is that we can learn more about one another through the things that we create.

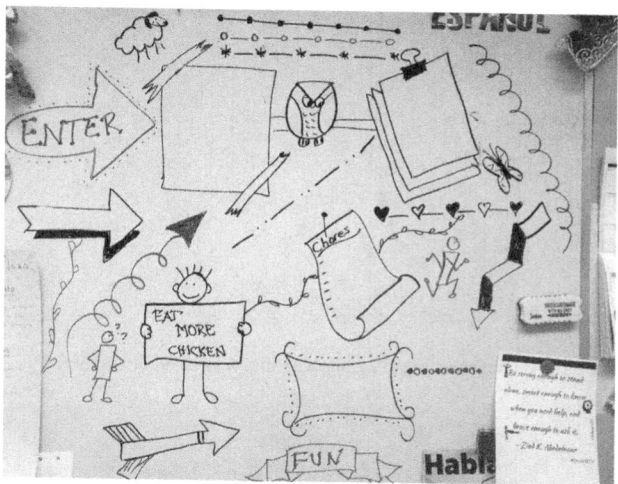

This is the board from the first day that I taught sketchnoting to
my eighth graders. To start, I followed Sylvia Duckworth's
drawings from her *How to Sketchnote Handbook*.

Sketchnoting is not only a fun activity, but one that can be applied in
many ways for learning. Even students who are not fans of drawing,
enjoy the opportunity to create something fun and different, and to
see what their classmates create. It will not take long for students to
make connections with their peers. By looking at the other drawings,
they will realize that they have more in common than they thought.
Some popular similarities are being fans of Netflix, YouTube, and
pizza. You will also see who loves drawing and who hopes to get the
activity over with and move on to the next thing. For more ideas,
check out the resources from Sylvia Duckworth. There are also some
sketchnotes and graphics displayed within this book, and you can find
many people on Twitter to follow by checking out the hashtag
#sketchnotes.

First day of teaching sketchnoting this year to eighth-graders.

Students created sketchnotes to teach about Digital Citizenship.

Create Together

Something that can make a big difference in classrooms is implementing station rotations. Station rotation is a model of instruction where students work through different learning activities at each "station" in the classroom. A good reference to learn about station rotations and blended learning is *Blended Learning in Action* (Tucker, Wycoff, & Green, 2017). During station rotations, teachers can facilitate one of the stations with direct instruction, use the time to work individually with students, or interact with each group throughout the class period. There are different models of station rotation such as groups of students rotate to each station on a fixed schedule in class or individual students working through stations at their own pace or a pace set by the teacher. The number of stations that I have used has ranged from between three and five, depending on class size. Although I did not know much about using station rotations at the time, I decided to give them a try in my own classroom a few years ago.

When I got rid of the rows of desks and created separate groups of desks around the room, it opened up more space for students to interact and work with peers they may not know very well. Students can be shy or hesitant to work with others. When we can connect with someone that we already know, it makes it easier to adapt to a new or uncomfortable situation. By creating these stations randomly, students can develop their interpersonal skills and become more comfortable in their learning environment.

Grouping students can be an issue. Deciding whether to allow students to choose their own groups is tricky. The best advice is to base it on the students you are working with, and maybe start by creating random groups. As a student, I found working in groups to be somewhat uncomfortable, whether or not I had to pick a partner or was assigned to a specific group. It can be awkward if you are the only one who doesn't find somebody to work with. Assigning random groups can help to alleviate some of those uncomfortable feelings, even though in life and for the future, students may face some of the same challenges and uncomfortable moments of not having a choice in collaborative work or not being chosen to participate. But we can help them by planning these activities and working along with them. When we foster relationship building in our classrooms, our students start to look for and offer to be partners with one another.

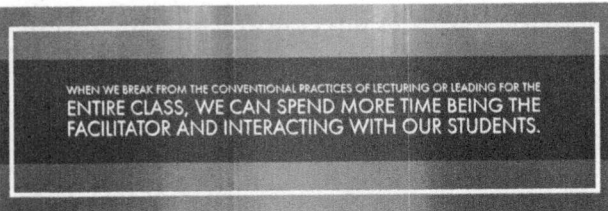

WHEN WE BREAK FROM THE CONVENTIONAL PRACTICES OF LECTURING OR LEADING FOR THE ENTIRE CLASS, WE CAN SPEND MORE TIME BEING THE FACILITATOR AND INTERACTING WITH OUR STUDENTS.

Getting Started

It can be easy to set up stations, depending on your classroom design. With station rotations, try to create groups of desks or "stations" in your classroom, with each station having a different activity. Get started by explaining how the movement through the rotations will work, provide guidelines, and just take a chance and see how it goes. Prepare a variety of learning activities to be used at each station. Try a mix of hands-on activities, with and without tech tools, and also offer the students the chance to come up with their own. Set up each station with the materials needed: use class resources, have students create their own, use tech tools, or set up a game. Deciding on the activities takes planning, especially when trying this for the first time. Don't let this stop you. Remember, we are all learners, and it is good for students to see that it is okay to take a risk by trying something new, to make mistakes, and to keep going. Giving up some control in the classroom is not easy, but the benefit is that it enables the teacher to facilitate and not drive learning, provide individualized instruction, and builds relationships that are the foundation of education today and for life.

WHEN WE BREAK from the conventional practices of lecturing or leading for the entire class, we can spend more time being the facilitator and interacting with our students. By stepping back, we allow students to build their skills and learn to self-assess, and we are more accessible to provide individualized instruction and the feedback they need. You will see with each passing week, students start to form their own learning networks, and your classroom will become a thriving learning community. You may even hear your students saying how much they enjoy being a part of a learning family.

Reflect

As educators, it is our responsibility to help facilitate peer connections to ensure that all students feel comfortable and welcome in our learning spaces. There are many ways to bring about these opportunities, and the best part is that as the teacher, we can and should join in as well. Students need to understand more than just *who* the teacher is; they deserve to understand what the teacher is about and understand our why. When we help students to develop these positive relationships, it fosters student engagement and academic achievement.

Ask yourself:

- How often do I get to engage in conversations with each of my students?
- Do students have time to be social in class while learning?
- What is one unconventional way that I can learn more about each student?

How often do I get to engage in conversations with each of my students?
Do students have time to be social in class while learning?
What is one unconventional way that I can learn more about each student?

Your Plan to Connect

As educators, forming relationships is critical to the success of students in our classrooms and schools. We need to help students develop the 21st Century skills of self-advocacy, collaboration, and cultural sensitivity, as well as incorporate social-emotional learning strategies in our teaching. It can be uncomfortable for some students to speak up, to ask for help, or to interact with their classmates, especially in a new classroom setting. Make it a point to help students feel a sense of belonging. Some of the ways that I have found effective for doing this include:

1. Be present. Greet all students as they enter the school and your classroom and as you pass them in the hallways.

2. Be intentional. Interact with each student every day. Learn who they are and let them know you too.

3. Be invested. Create learning experiences for students to collaborate and learn and grow together.

#THRIVEinEDU

Now it's up to you to work on those relationship-building activities in your classroom and your school. Try one of these ideas or create your own relationship builder and share it out on Twitter using the hashtag #THRIVEinEDU.

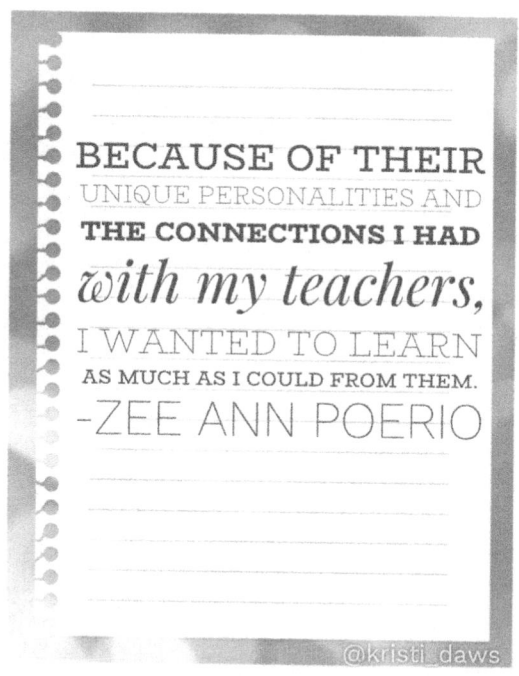

Quote shared by Zee Ann Poerio from my book *In Other Words.* Graphic by Kristi Daws

2 CONNECTING THE FAMILY OF LEARNING

A Path to Family Engagement

In the movie, *Ferris Bueller's Day Off*, Ferris, a high school senior, pretends to be sick and stays home because he has his own plan for the day. You can tell that he is crafty when it comes to his planning, as he manages to fool his parents and even sets up a way to fake a conversation when a phone call is received. The high school principal, Mr. Rooney, and his secretary attempt to contact Ferris's parents by phone, but instead reach the recording of Ferris sounding sick. Ferris's message nearly succeeds, but the answering machine and the message glitch. It does not take long until Mr. Rooney becomes even more suspicious of Ferris and decides to head out to look for him in town. Right before leaving, he receives a phone call from the father of Ferris's girlfriend Sloane, who asks that Sloane be dismissed from school. Mr. Rooney sees Sloane leave with her "father," who is actually Ferris in disguise. The teenagers then head into town for the day, narrowly avoiding run-ins with Ferris's father and Mr. Rooney.

❄

JUST THINKING about these few scenes in the movie, we can tell that the school does not have a real clear understanding of how to contact the parents, or what the parents look like. This cannot happen in schools today. We need to know the parents and families of our students. When Mr. Rooney is speaking to Sloane's "father" on the phone, he does not pick up on the fact that it is not the voice of an adult, but rather a teenager disguising his voice. We must be intentional in knowing the parents and families of our students because their well-being and safety are our greatest responsibilities.

So, what is the lesson we can learn from Ferris? We need to fully invest in learning as much about our students and their families as we can. Our relationships center on doing what is best for students and providing a well-rounded system of support for them and their families. This means that we must know how to reach them, recognize them in public, and make it a priority to consistently work toward building a relationship with them by connecting through telephone calls and email at a minimum. However, we should also make time to meet them in person. Sometimes home visits might be necessary, as Mr. Rooney paid a visit to Ferris's home to check on him. We are often called upon to help families in times of need or to check in, and we must make ourselves available for them. It is important to let them know that they have our support and that we are dedicated to doing what is best for the children in our school.

Let's Connect

One of the most important responsibilities for educators is to facilitate ongoing communication with the families in our schools. We need to have a plan for sharing the news about what is happening in our classrooms and with our students. We must strive for family engagement and create partnerships between school, home, and the community, so together, we can provide a network of support for all students. When we have a system for fostering these partnerships, it will build rapport and establish more meaningful and personal connections within the school community. Together we can work to provide a structure that will positively impact student achievement and well-being.

We must be intentional in reaching out to our students and their families, become aware of their needs, and develop an understanding of their prior experiences with schools. We might ask families to express any frustrations with prior experiences and share preferences for methods of communicating. When we have information like this, it helps us know how to best provide for the specific needs of each family.

To do this, we must actively explore best practices for opening up the lines of communication and providing access to the resources our students need to be successful. The best support that we can provide for students does not depend on only what we as teachers provide to them in the classroom. It extends to the support that we can offer for their home life because we are invested in caring for the whole child.

When we understand some of the frustrations, we can develop specific strategies that are aimed at reducing and ultimately eliminating any barriers to communication. From parents who have shared their concerns and frustrations, some of the common barriers to family engagement are time, lack of resources, and inability to attend school events because of work-related issues. Understanding the diverse needs of the families and students in our school system is crucial so that we can help our families to be involved and connected.

Let's Make Ourselves Available

Think about how often you have interacted with the parents of your students. Do you feel comfortable saying that the methods you have in place are working well, or are there areas in which you could improve? Do you find yourself wishing for more time and opportunities to connect? We must have reliable ways for all families to access information, to receive class updates, and to be able to ask for help or resources when they need them. Imagine the frustration of a parent who is trying to help their child but cannot reach the teacher and does not know what resources are available to assist. The families of our students need to feel as supported as our students, so we must consider what we can do to help those parents and students connect with their school family.

FOR YEARS, the conventional ways that teachers connected with parents were phone calls, parent-teacher conferences, or letters sent by mail or home with students. Of course, with the development of a variety of technology tools, especially email correspondence, we can facilitate a faster and easier way to make these connections happen more often. However, not everyone checks their email as often as some of us may. Personally, I am always connected and feel compelled to respond as soon as I possibly can, often immediately after receiving an email. But what do we do when families may not have access to email or the Internet even? Or when families do not rely on email as much as we do? With fewer homes having a real home phone anymore, and letters possibly getting lost in the mail, how can we make sure that our messages are being received? How can we facilitate better communication when the conventional methods are seemingly either not enough anymore or not as time-efficient? Or effective?

Just Ask

The most important first step is finding out what communication preferences are for our parents and the families of our students. We need to be aware of any families whose home language is not English. There are many ways to do this that will promote a home to school community. One common method is sending home the traditional handout that includes course information, but add to it by including a link to an online survey for parents. Invest more time in learning about them, ask for email addresses, phone numbers, and even preferred contact times, and then ask the student to return the paper to you. We will have that information accessible in the traditional format; however, by also creating a survey, we can get additional information such as asking for family preferences when it comes to calls, giving regular updates and news, or simply letting them know about specific student progress throughout the year.

WITH TIME BEING SO CRITICAL, especially when we need to convey messages to families that are of a more urgent matter, related to the student's progress or perhaps something that would require an actual meeting, we still need to be able to make that contact right away. Several options exist that are not entirely the conventional ways that many of us have utilized, whether as the student or as a parent, but which facilitate a quicker exchange of information that is at least a starting point. If there needs to be a meeting set up or call made, using some of these ideas helps to begin that process more quickly. The best part about these options is that the messages will be accessible, and the information can be posted online and made available to students and parents. Families will be more engaged in what is going on in the classroom and become more involved in communicating regarding the updates from the class.

One thing to remember is to make sure to provide parents and families with enough details and guidelines as to how you plan to use these tools and formats to facilitate conversations. Definitely convey the purpose you have for using these as opposed to the other forms of communication that might be typically used by other teachers and classrooms. We can also count on administrative staff to help, as they are often the first point of contact that families reach when communicating with the school. They form relationships with the families and can provide additional support as needed. Having multiple options for sharing the news and the happenings from the classroom is very important. Not only will it facilitate a better relationship between home and school, but it will also add to the technology skills of families as well.

A Plan to Connect

Many wonderful things happen in our classrooms every day, and it is important to share this information promptly. The world needs to hear and be a part of our school's story. Parents may ask children about their school day, hoping to find out what they learned. But often, the child might respond, "nothing." However, considering students spend roughly eight hours a day in school, taking anywhere between five and eight courses, we know they learned something. They probably learned a lot because school is full of opportunities for learning. Maybe the real answer is not that they didn't learn *anything;* it might be that they prefer not to share the information with parents. As educators, we need to encourage students to communicate with their families about what occurs in school, and we need to set up ways for students to open up more to share their learning experiences.

OPPORTUNITIES TO LEARN ARE EVERYWHERE. Students learn by interacting with peers, through conversations with teachers and administrators, and by pursuing their interests through activities at school. We have to help our students understand that learning is an ongoing process and is not confined to a certain time and place. We need to help students become more aware of different ways to learn. Our responsibility as educators is to help them become comfortable and actively engaged in sharing what they have been working on in school. Parents benefit from understanding the work that their child does in school and can help if needed, but more importantly, they become connected with the school experience of their child. Being able to include parents in the learning facilitates collaboration between home and school. Homework assignments or projects assigned could be worked on at home, involving parents in helping to support the student in their work. Creating a space to communicate with parents helps with relationship building and fosters the home-to-school connection that is beneficial to student growth.

Trying some of these ideas will help you to share information about what is going on in the classroom with the families. Send updates home regularly. Communicate specific information about the child to the parents. Have face-to-face conversations or talk on the phone with family members to interpret tone and ensure the message is shared, and concerns are addressed. If time is an obstacle, consider digital options.

BEFORE DECIDING ON METHODS, I recommend administering a survey to invite parents and families to express preferences for using digital tools. Be sure to include a brief explanation, such as the name of the tool, intended use, age levels, privacy, and security-related information. Let parents know these factors ahead of time, so they can decide what works best for them and their child. Once you have this information, decide how to proceed and keep in mind you may change from your original plan, based on the feedback that you receive. It may end up that you use a mix of methods to meet the needs and interests of families. Also, consider any language translation needs, and make sure families have access to the right technology, and be prepared to address these.

1. **Communication Tools**: One of the best ways to start is by figuring out which communication tools work best for your learning environment. Depending on the grade level you teach, specific tools are more effective than others. Consider methods and benefits of sharing photos, videos, and student work. Some social media platforms like Facebook, Instagram, and Twitter can be used to post updates and are useful for sharing with an audience such as the

school community. LinkedIn can help make professional connections. However, be sure to comply with your school or district policies.

For sharing class information safely and privately with families, consider tools such as BloomzApp or Remind. For more options, a platform such as ParentSquare helps to connect families with needed information and facilitate a holistic approach. When using tools like these, parents and students can be part of the class and have access to the announcements when they are made. These tools facilitate vital communication between home and school and promote family engagement in learning. Although tools may change, the concept remains: leverage technology to bring families into the classroom and be part of the learning journey.

2. **Class Blog or Website:** Some teachers enjoy having a "space" where they can post resources and updates about their classroom. The conventional way has been a designated space in the classroom where assignments and learning goals are posted for the day, and materials are accessible in trays or file folders or some combination. However, what can we do when students are not in school and are unable to get these materials? How do we prevent the lost opportunity for learning? And also, how can we facilitate sharing these materials with families?

Many options are available. Some are easy to use because they have a basic design, while others are more detailed and may include options like multimedia. We still have conventional ways like phone calls, notes sent home, and email. However, more interactive ways to create a virtual classroom space exist. Why not involve students in sharing by using a blog or a class website?

Easy-to-use tools such as **Edmodo**, **Google Classroom**, **Kidblog**, **Seesaw**, and **Padlet** are options. Inviting parents or students to participate is easy to do. When families have a centralized online site available where they can stay informed of updates, send questions, or access additional class materials, they can become engaged and involved. Families can be included in daily activities, and these tools foster important connections between school and home. These online tools also give families convenient access to information.

3. Video Tools: Technology has fostered opportunities to more effectively communicate within our classroom and beyond our classroom walls. Some of these tools enable students to create a product that demonstrates their learning and serves as a way for students, parents, and teachers to learn about one another and communicate effectively. Ordinarily, when students create projects or do an activity to show their learning, perhaps the only people who see their work are teachers and classmates. However, we now can offer students opportunities to share their work publicly.

Ask students how often they share work with their families, and you may find that it does not happen often. Papers become misplaced or just don't make it home. By using video tools such as **Flipgrid** or WeVideo, we can share news and student work with families. Here are some ideas:

- Have students record videos to share learning.
- Invite parents to record videos in response to a theme or class lesson.
- Create videos to share class updates.
- Have students create online updates or school news programs for families.

Videos offer a way for parents to interact and see what the students are learning.

Using tools like **Buncee** can be a creative way to share news and engage families. The addition of Immersive Reader to Buncee promotes accessibility for students and families for creating and sharing work. Here are a few ideas:

- Create presentations and record a video within it to share with classmates and families.

- Have students use Buncee to create a class newsletter! Imagine how fun it would be to get a newsletter created and narrated by students! Students can take turns recording and adding information to each slide, producing a final class video newsletter.
- Create invitations and flyers to invite families and the school community to events.

In addition to these tools, teachers can create screencasts with applications like **Screencastify** and **Educreations**. In screencasts, teachers can explain a lesson step-by-step, and once shared with parents, they can help their child at home.

Also, consider recording videos for weekly announcements and providing details related to special events happening in the school. Also, why not engage students in creating these!

Further, explore using Artificial Intelligence and have students work together to create a class chatbot. You can create a chatbot that can be accessed by students and parents as a reminder for how to solve a problem, explain a concept, or provide instructions on how to complete an assignment.

By using video tools in these ways, we create a supportive connection for our students, opening a way to unite the home and school communities. Videos serve as an authentic way for students to share their learning, explain something in their own words, or create a digital portfolio. Also, consider asking families to record video introductions so they can learn about one another too!

4. **Welcome to School!** Typically throughout the year, parents and families are welcomed into the school. Back-to-School Night, an open house, and parent-teacher conferences offer opportunities to meet families, engage in conversations, and connect in person. However, these events don't necessarily provide enough time for fully getting to know students and their families. So why not create your own "welcome to school" event, for example, lunch with the

teacher, an after-school coffee meet-and-greet event, or a student showcase inviting families to see the work of students. Create a gallery walk and use Augmented and Virtual Reality tools to make a virtual tour! Have students available to interact with the families. Imagine the excitement when families see students use tools like Flipgrid AR to record their thoughts or a short presentation! Consider the awe of parents scanning a QR code to view student work!

OF COURSE, we want to make sure that each family has the chance to be involved in these events, so be sure to ask for availability and schedule more than one event so each family can find one that meets their schedule. When we are intentional about planning for families, we can provide the right opportunities that enable each family to participate. Look into your school community for a nearby center, accessible without transportation, and perhaps that offers childcare services. Find out if any families need translators or other services to help with accessing and exchanging information. To add more to these events, involve students in creating a video of the activity that can be shared with the community and with any families that might have missed out, so they can still feel involved and connected. Let's truly engage families and build our learning family for our students!

Your Classroom Story

Making time to connect with and understand our students is critical to their growth. In order to provide what each of our students and their families need, we must make ourselves available and set up a means to communicate that works for them. Including families in these communications is critical today so we can build a bridge between our classrooms and our communities. It isn't about the technology, but in this case, many tools are available that help us to resolve the challenges of time and location for interacting. We just need to think about what it is we are trying to communicate and what will work the best for members of our learning community.

Knowing that we need to actively communicate and having tools to help us is not enough. We also cannot forget to consider any issues of accessibility that families may have and that our students may also face when they are not with us in our classrooms. Digital equity is critical, and we need to make it a priority to learn about any barriers our students and their families may face. We need to bring our best selves to our classrooms and our schools each day. We do this by being intentional in preparing for our students and creating transformational learning opportunities in our classrooms. When educators seize the opportunity to try new things and continue to grow, they provide their best selves for those they lead and learn with.

Digital equity is more than just making sure that our students have access to devices. We need to make sure that families have access to the technology and resources that will enable them to support our students when they are at home. As teachers, we also need to stay current with new ideas and resources that will benefit our students and make sure that we have strategies in place to work through any challenges related to digital equity. A helpful resource for educators is *Closing the Gap: Digital Equity Strategies for the K-12 Classroom* (Thomas, Howard, & Schaffer, 2019), part of a series of books aimed at providing the right information for educational stakeholders.

There is no substitute for having personal conversations with parents, but we know that time is not always available or mutually convenient. In these situations, we can rely on technology to serve a purpose that is beneficial for student learning.

Reflect

Think about the different forms of communication that you have used during your teaching career. How did you make the decision of which form to use, whether it be a letter that you sent home with each student, an email that you sent to the group of parents, or phone calls only made on an as-needed basis? Perhaps the best way to proceed is to think about whether you believe that the method of communication you have been using is working. If not, or if it could be improved (it always can), then try an alternate format. Try something different, and see if you notice any positive changes and continue to build from there. Share your experience with your colleagues and Professional Learning Network (PLN). Sometimes we all need a little push in the right direction when it comes to our practice.

Consider your own practice. How often did you send messages home, and what method of communication did you use? And for each communication, did you receive a response, or was it solely for informational purposes without expectation of a response? It might be beneficial to create a class page where you can provide links to supplement content covered to class, adding in resources, and sending class updates. A virtual space where families can find everything they might need would be beneficial, but also have a backup format for sharing more pressing matters of communication with parents. Use some questions to guide you as you decide what will work best for your students and families. Consider: Did you find that when you would send an email, you did not receive a response? Or did you leave voicemail messages after making a phone call home, but not receive a phone call in return? These are a few things to consider, and it may require that you use different formats with some parents. It is important to find what works best for each member of your learning community.

MAKE the decision to try one of these strategies this week. When we are intentional about making those connections, and we know and understand our families and their needs, the choice to act is much easier. You can start your plan today:

- Create a survey to get to know your families and their preferences. Send the information home with students in a letter or in an email, or even both. We want to make sure the first message is received by the families so we can develop our communication plan.
- Choose one of the platforms (Buncee, Flipgrid, Kidblog, Padlet, Synth) to create a more interactive welcome message, a post about the happenings in your classroom, or something coming up that families should know about. Share it out with families and reflect on the feedback or responses you receive.
- Look at the school calendar and select a few dates to use for the "Welcome to School" events. Once you have chosen a few, stagger the times on those days so that families can find at least one event that meets their schedule. Make it more engaging by creating an invitation, possibly even having students create the invitation.

#THRIVEinEDU

Try any one of these ideas to set up a different line of communication with your families. Give it some time and see what improvements you notice, and also be sure to ask parents for their responses. Please share your experience and tips using the hashtag #THRIVEinEDU.

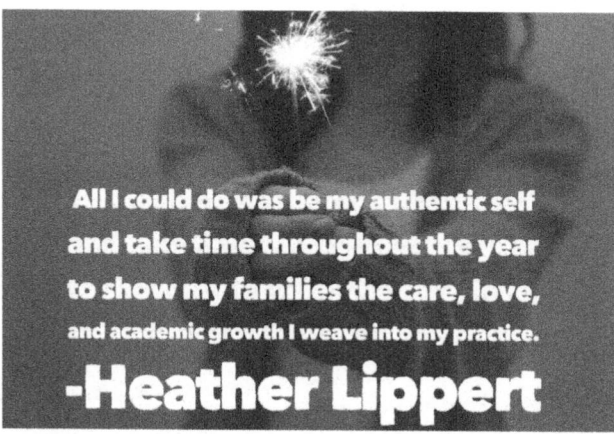

All I could do was be my authentic self and take time throughout the year to show my families the care, love, and academic growth I weave into my practice.

-Heather Lippert

Quote from Heather Lippert's vignette in my book, *In Other Words*, image by Kristi Daws

A New Classroom Experience

Do you remember your days in elementary school? Did you have your own desk where you could keep all of your books and class materials, plus some other things you added just because it was yours? It was a space that you could make your own. Did you have anything special in there? Maybe some candy, a pencil case, a stuffed animal or toy, depending on your grade. (Maybe that was just me.) There was something about having my own space that made learning fun and comfortable. It was my own secret compartment. Or how about in junior or senior high school, did you have a locker decked out with accessories, organizers, pictures, and more? Even though you rarely had much time to get there, it was still a space to stop, gather your thoughts, catch your breath, and serve as your comfort zone. In any setting, we all have ways to make ourselves more comfortable. Sometimes routines are good, and knowing what to count on helps, but we also need to explore ways to find and adapt to new experiences.

HAVING a space to call one's own is important no matter what your role is or what you do. Have you gone to a conference, or participated in a PD session, where you first scanned the room, strategically thinking about where to place yourself that would give you room to work, with a path to exit if needed? A space that you could make into your own comfort zone? Maybe even seeking a space that would give you some privacy, allowing you to be involved in the session but work on something else at the same time? What happens when you find that perfect spot, set yourself up comfortably, only to be asked to move to the front, or to a different table, or even worse, you are told where to go? How does it make you feel?

Now apply this to your own experience as a student. Can you remember what it was like in elementary school? Did you have assigned seats, and were desks lined up in rows? Did you move from class to class, or did you stay in the same classroom, and only the teachers moved? Were you seated alphabetically? While this helped you get to know the people whose names came before and after yours in the alphabet, it did not help you get to know the other students in the classroom. Or how about in high school, were you assigned to work with a certain group in physical education and consumer science classes, or maybe paired up with a lab partner in science? Do you recall having the same partner and being in the same location in the classroom every day? If any of this sounds familiar, it's because it is the most common scenario and what has traditionally been done when it comes to classroom setup and the design of learning spaces over the years.

The traditional classroom setup meant that the desks were lined up in rows, the teacher was at the front center, the students were focused on the teacher, and in most cases, and definitely not a personal favorite, students were arranged alphabetically. And of course, we can't forget the comfort, or lack of it, depending on furniture styles available at each of these grade levels. For some, the furniture may have always been the same. Standard sled desks or in more recent years, styles may have changed to more of a flexible and definitely more comfortable learning space and experience. Either way, there was likely a structure to the room, and a bulk of the class time was spent with students sitting and listening. Does this compare at all to the professional development sessions that we as teachers have to be a part of? Think about your own reaction to those situations and then compare it with the experiences that your students might be having in your own classroom. Is there something that you might want to change? And if so, what is stopping you?

Maybe it is due to the room structure, or perhaps because of uncertainty about how to make changes. What can we do about schools and classrooms where there are no options for flexible furniture, and the learning space does not offer enough to really mix things up enough for students? If you think back to the number of hours that students spend sitting in classrooms in grades K through 12 (around 11,700 hours), that is a really long time to stay in the same space and only move, in most cases, whenever the bell signals to do so. It is time to break away from the conventional and do something different. Learning needs to be active and social. Think about the changes you would have liked during your years as a student and make them in your own classroom.

Let's go!

Let's Learn on the Move

Sitting all day can be exhausting! There should be movement and opportunities for students to be more active in classrooms. Make a few changes and give students an experience doing something different than simply the "sit and get," a practice which many educators experience during professional development sessions. If you have had these types of experiences and don't find them to be too favorable, then why would you want your students to experience the same thing? I wish I would have asked myself this question many years ago, when I felt compelled to line the desks up in rows and to assign seats for my students...so much time spent drawing the charts and then checking off attendance as students entered the room. What is your classroom like? Are students lined up alphabetically? What other structured classroom design has become part of your teaching practice? Can you reach each student without having to walk around your whole classroom? This is important to consider.

I stayed away from alphabetical assignments because I did not like that system when I was a student. Being seated alphabetically makes students interact with the same classmates each day, rather than being able to collaborate with different peers. By not changing seats often enough, students may not have an interactive classroom experience, which is ideal for learning. Students in the front of the classroom may feel like they are getting too much attention, feel uncomfortable because they are in a prime location for questioning, or feel like they have to actively pay attention and are only engaging to comply. Whereas the students in the back of the room may not get enough attention, especially if the teacher's movement is limited based on the classroom space, or the teaching practices used are more of a lecture format for students to "sit and get." There are so many benefits to mixing seats up to allow all students to interact with one another in the classroom, but more importantly, to have greater access to the teacher.

"If your students didn't have to be there would you be teaching to an empty room?"

DAVE BURGESS, TEACH LIKE A PIRATE

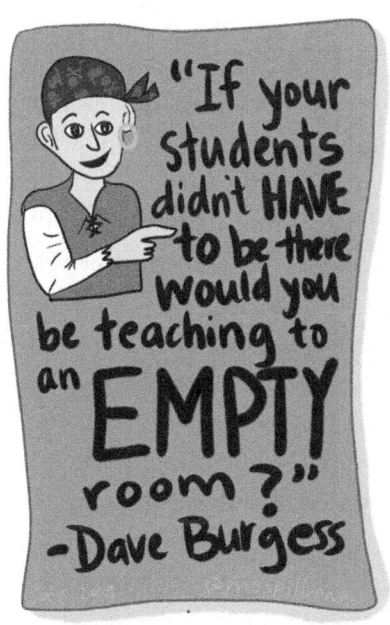

So how can educators break from that traditional, sometimes restrictive classroom structure? The rigid structure which limits interactions between teacher and student and between student and student because of real or perceived barriers set up in the room. Learning today needs to take place in an environment that promotes building the skills that will prepare students for the future. A place to learn the content but also develop the ability to collaborate, problem-solve, communicate, and become the creators and not just consumers in the classroom. There are so many quick ways to get started, especially which promote more student choice in the classroom, helping students feel more valued and empowered in their learning. Classes shouldn't always have students sitting, passively learning, and only engaging with the teacher occasionally and with peers, even less frequently.

ALL STUDENTS SHOULD BE INVOLVED in making decisions about the classroom and learning spaces. When we are intentional with involving students in class decisions, they will feel more at home in the classroom and excited about what each new day of learning brings. We make this possible by offering students the chance to decide some of the routines, rhythms, and learning spaces. It may not seem like these little steps and interactions will have an impact, but they do. In many personal experiences, when issues arose that could very easily have gone in a negative direction, either leading to a conflict, to students shutting down, or worse, having a major impact on the classroom culture, the one thing that made a difference was showing students that they are valued and that we are in this together. Setting up our classroom and working together to make decisions left each member feeling valued and welcomed in the learning space. It is okay to follow the traditional or conventional way of doing things like setting up the layout of your classroom, decorating your walls, and being the sole decision-maker when it comes to rules and procedures. Following a consistent routine helps for building a positive culture and safe learning space. But it's even better and way more empowering when we break tradition and implement some unconventional ideas. If we give the students more opportunities to design their learning space, to co-create with teachers, and to be part of an effort of cultivating positive, responsive, and supportive relationships between all learners, we build a thriving learning environment.

SOMETHING TO KEEP in mind is that for the most part, many students don't mind sitting on the floor or cramming into a small area of the room. As uncomfortable as it may look, that is where they find the most comfort, especially if they can work with their peers. Sometimes it is simply because they can get out of the uncomfortable seats that they spend so much time in every day. Let them decide and go with it. Remember, there may be times where you have to kneel or sit on the floor or lean up against the wall to interact with the students. The idea is to help students become more comfortable in their space, and their chosen space might be not as comfortable for you. Sit with them, wherever they choose, and gain some new insight into how students want to learn. Either way, it's unconventional (for you and for them), but with so much potential for learning and growing together.

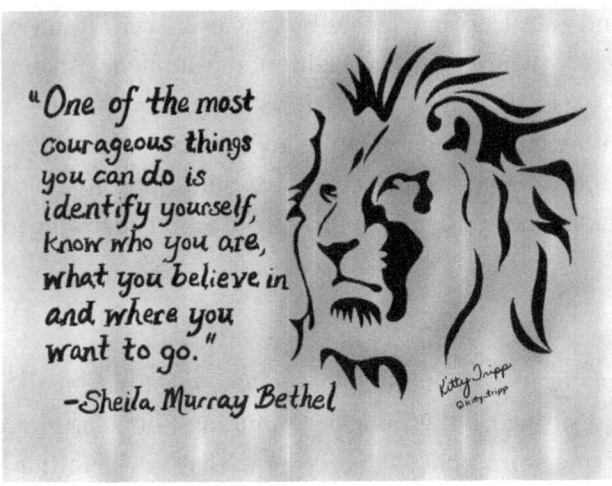

"One of the most courageous things you can do is identify yourself, know who you are, what you believe in and where you want to go."
—Sheila Murray Bethel

Image created by Kitty Tripp for the book *In Other Words*

A Plan to Diverge from Tradition

1) Classroom Setting and Appearance. Traditionally, teachers are the ones who prepare the classroom, decorate the walls, determine the classroom layout, and set up everything to welcome students to school. Instead, why not give students the chance to design the layout, display their work, write their own quotes, and make the learning space their own? Students will feel a greater sense of belonging when they have contributed to something and feel valued. Classrooms should be warm and welcoming spaces where students feel comfortable and connected. Involve students in making decisions about how to set up the learning space.

In many of my years of teaching, I used some of the traditional methods that I had experienced as a student. I made all of the decisions about the classroom setup, and my students took their places as directed. It's time to move past this, especially when students express how boring it is to sit in the same space or do not have any opportunities to move around in the classroom. While many of us spent years doing the exact same thing the students of today are doing, that does not mean that the old way is best. Of course, for certain classes, teachers might prefer a specific structure because it works better. Depending on the content area and grade level you teach, you may find it works best for classroom management to have the desks lined up in rows with each student in their assigned place. This format might be best for courses where students need to use a lot of materials and safety is a concern. You want to make sure your learning spaces are mindful of these needs.

Look closely around your classroom space. What do you have on the walls, on the bulletin boards, and in other areas of your classroom? Are you displaying things that *you* believe are important? Are you displaying student work? Or are your classroom walls bare to avoid possible distractions? Really think about these questions and decide what can benefit your students. Maybe sharing their work with other students who enter the classroom or having their unique interests represented by the designs and visuals displayed in the room will enhance their learning experience. It can make for a good conversation and get the students moving. Some of the most creative ideas come from students, and many times, they have a clever idea of how to design the classroom space. Give students time to evaluate the space and work with you to create an amazing space for everyone.

Things to Consider

Do you have to use rows of desks in your classroom? Is there any flexibility at all in the type of furniture in your room? Even with the most uncomfortable furniture, consider options for flexibility. If you try to come up with ideas and you're not having any luck, challenge the students to find a solution. Be prepared in case they decide on an intriguing idea that just may not be feasible. A few years ago, my senior homeroom gladly accepted the challenge to rearrange the desks, and their solution was to push them against the back wall facing the cabinet doors. While I appreciated their creativity, their plan just did not work. But it gave us a starting point to build on. Find a middle ground and create a space that works for everyone.

The best advice is to design your room in a way, so all students have access to the resources and the help that they need whenever they need it. Lined up desks, with five or six in each row, does not offer that opportunity. Try something different, something unconventional, and see how it goes. Worst case scenario? You have to move the furniture back to where it was. But that just means it's time to ask students again and come up with a new plan, and one of the enjoyable parts of learning. Try, fail, think, try again, reflect.

2) **"Chalk and talk."** Have you been guilty of doing the "chalk and talk" in your classroom? Of course, not many classrooms still have the original chalkboards with chalk, erasers, and all of that dust, but the concept is still the same. Are you standing in front of the room, writing on the board, and basically talking to the board? Let's get real, we need to make the most of our class time together, and it should not be spent simply writing on the board and talking *at* the students.

So how can we talk less and listen more, and beyond that, how can we get students to do more talking and ask more questions? To start, center the learning at each of their desks within small groups, or however your classroom is set up. We need to push ourselves out of the way to allow students to create and determine how to spend their class time. Not that there's necessarily anything wrong with "chalk and talk." It's just that if it's the teacher who's doing most of the talking and writing, they are also doing most of the learning. Think of how well you know the content you are teaching. We need to give students more ways to be involved. Try these ideas instead:

- Have students go to the board or use small dry-erase boards at their desks to respond to questions.
- Have groups grab paper and markers and collaborate on different activities.
- Use a digital tool to work through problems or come up with ideas to share, teach, and work with one another.

When we make it our mission to involve students more, we generate authentic learning and provide possibilities for students to own their learning.

3) **Movement and Music: No Noise, Loud is bad!** Turn that music down. Learning only occurs in quiet, focused environments, right? *Maybe* in a traditional classroom, but in an unconventional classroom, music has power and can be used in many ways.

Let's Get This Learning Party Started

Music can be helpful for welcoming people into a new space, lightening the mood, finding ways to relax, providing musical motivation to complete a task, or for exercise and well-being. Music is beneficial in many ways. When I play a song, I see the impact on students as they enter the room. The mood shifts to movement, it creates a more positive vibe. Playing music while students work, or letting students listen to their own music, creates an upbeat classroom environment. It also offers a unique and more personal way to learn about students. Try playing random music. Choose music that is not related to the class, perhaps from another era, a show tune, or anything in between. Create a survey to ask students for ideas to build a class playlist, thereby giving students a voice and valuing their musical tastes. It will be fun when students hear their song playing as they arrive to class. They might even start dancing! But of course, first check the lyrics of songs that you do not know, to ensure they are appropriate and classroom friendly.

Let's Compare Playlists

Think back to some of your favorite songs growing up. Maybe some of them were one-hit wonders, and when you heard them, your mood lifted, and you started singing and dancing. Create the same energy for your students. Cue up some random songs on a Monday morning (or every morning), turn the volume up, and greet students at the door to welcome them in with the music and positivity. Besides the fact that students will come in trying to guess the song that is playing, it is another opportunity to share experiences and maybe find a song that was popular at the time when you were the same age as your students. Put one of your old-time favorites on and have students compare it to music today. Are there any similarities? Are there differences? What do your students think of your favorites? Do they wonder how in the world you listened to that? It might be similar to what you think about their music style choices today.

TAKE a look around as students enter the room and see if you notice anything.

- Are your students dancing their way into the classroom?
- Do they seem happier? Is there a different kind of a vibe in the room?
- Do you notice more smiles as they enter your class?

Go beyond the doors of your classroom. Spread that energy into the halls and get more students and even your colleagues pumped up for learning. Maybe it's music that you need to get things livened up a bit and start each class with some positive energy!

Let's Write a Theme Song

Music has been shown to have positive effects on amplifying the learning potential of our students. Think back to some of the different mnemonics you might have learned during your years of schooling, whether related to a class or perhaps for music lessons, a sport, or something that you just made up on your own. How many songs can you think of that tied into the content you were learning in school, and that you still remember? (Especially the ones that can seem really quite bizarre at times, but that's exactly what makes them so authentic and beneficial for learning.) Making the learning personal to us by connecting with music can lead to more meaningful connections with the content and our classmates.

An interesting way to add to your instructional materials and tap into the creativity of students is to have them create their own rhymes or write a song. Provide examples and have students select a related vocabulary list, names of famous people, events in history, mathematical or science equations, or anything related to the content. You can use it as another opportunity to focus on building peer relationships and social-emotional learning skills by having students work in pairs or small groups.

Rhyme Time

The goal is to create a song or rhyme to use as a mnemonic device for students to practice and retain the content in a meaningful way. Give it a twist by asking students to suggest songs for background music by having them write titles on notecards. A fun way to mix it up is by having students select a card and create a new song based on the song that they receive. Students can then perform their musical selections in class, or to accommodate student level of comfort, try using one of the video response or voice recording tools like Flipgrid or Synth. Such student creations add more authentic learning experiences and classroom resources.

Let's Move!

We know many students typically spend the majority of their school day sitting in assigned seats, listening to lectures, or working independently and do not always have time to interact with peers, move around the classroom, or do more than consume content. Students become passive learners, and learning is limited to their own personal space in the room. Depending on the room setup, students can be isolated from one another and the teacher. As a result, student engagement and motivation can suffer. Students can become disengaged if the teacher spends too much time talking, and students have limited opportunities to move around, work with peers, and take control of their learning. I had been doing this in my classroom for years.

Yet movement can easily be added to the classroom. Break the activities for the day into sections and give students the option to move into a learning space in the classroom, or possibly in the hallway, where they may feel more comfortable. Some students prefer to sit or lay on the floor. I've been asked this for years, and many times in the past, I said no. However, I have changed my thinking and realize that sometimes, this is what works better for some students. A word of caution, be prepared for some strange looks as your colleagues or other students walk by and see students scattered around in small groups lying on the floor, sitting on desks, or even standing: they may question whether learning is happening. There is, just more powerful learning in unconventional places!

GIVE it a go and see where the students end up. Maybe they will even venture out into the hallway to have their own quiet space to work within their groups while others may stay in their regular seats. We don't know until we try, so run with it and see what happens. It might go really well, or you might have to rethink a little and create some guidelines. Students might need reminders to watch voice levels if working outside of the classroom, and to be careful when sitting around the classroom so as to not interfere with traffic moving in and around the room.

The main idea is not to be afraid to break away from the traditional or conventional setup of your classroom. When we take a chance, we amplify possibilities for student collaborations and break away from the sit and get.

Joy for Learning

The most important element is to involve students in determining how the classroom is set up. Adding music and movement into the classroom can excite students about learning. Of course, with any new method, we should start by asking ourselves, "why?" What are our goals, what do we hope to accomplish by making changes? When we take time to have conversations, ask for ideas, and open ourselves to feedback, we can provide the best learning space for our students.

Reflect

Consider student opinions in the discussion of when to add music to class and what types to include. Create a playlist based on student recommendations and rotate it during the week or on certain days. It's about choices and helping students to feel valued in the classroom by working to create different experiences for them. When we are intentional about improving our learning space, students are excited about learning and less focused on the clock and when the bell is going to ring.

Quick Ideas

Choose one of these ideas and try it for a week or two. To see what a difference it makes, create a survey or talk with your students and ask for some suggestions. Determine if there are any other ways you can change the setup of the classroom or anything else that can add to the learning space.

1. Create a short survey and distribute it to your students to find out what they would listen to if they could. Look over the responses before creating a class playlist to make sure that it is appropriate for all students.
2. Think about songs that were popular during your life at the same age and make your own playlist to mix in and share with

them. On those days, set aside a few minutes just to talk about the music because it's likely they will have questions about it. You can find a way to tie it into the content material as well— it just takes a little bit of creative and unconventional thinking.

3. Take a good look at your classroom space as well as any areas right outside of your room. Make sure you have access to check in on students if they choose to go out into a different space to work. If students are going to work on an activity in class or in small groups that might be difficult to do on the student desks, encourage students to find a space in the room where they think it will be easier to work together. Then take the time to walk around and interact with each group. It is probably a good idea to ask how those spaces are working for them as well. And then the next time, have students choose a different space, just to find their true comfortable space. The main idea is to build comfort and collaboration and to give students the chance to lead.

#THRIVEinEDU

Think you have come up with a really great playlist that represents a variety of musical interests of both you and the students? Does it seem to spread positivity, bring smiles to the faces of your students, and spread into the halls of your school? Share it by using the hashtag #THRIVEinEDU and ask for some feedback or suggestions to add to that playlist. We can "trend the positive" together!

Did you have students choose to work in some really peculiar places that you thought would totally not work but worked out really well for them? Share out some photos or ideas; we learn from sharing our stories and experiences. Learning can happen anywhere.

In the movie *Freedom Writers,* Hilary Swank portrayed real-life teacher Erin Gruwell, who begins her first teaching job in an inner-city school in Los Angeles. She tries to teach literature to a group of not quite receptive students and becomes frustrated at the challenge of involving her students in learning. She also meets with resistance by colleagues for trying to provide resources like books for her students. A transition begins after she intercepts a drawing and overhears comments about racism in the class. She uses this to begin teaching about the Holocaust and help the students make their own connections. She purchased journals for her students, who then began to write and share their own stories. She succeeded because she worked to understand each student, build relationships, and show them that they mattered. She taught them that in spite of their lack of confidence, or society's beliefs, they could succeed and learn in their own way. She broke away from the standard teaching methods, and instead focused less on teaching the "content," and more on teaching the student and making a connection with their world.

BEING a student brings with it a lot of pressure—pressure to fit in with peers, to balance class schedules, to make the grade, and to plan for the future. Life as a student can be full of wonderful experiences and growth, but can bring many challenges. Students want to be accepted, to know that they matter, and will have equal opportunities to succeed. There is so much competition in education: trying to achieve higher scores for college admission, aiming for academic honors, and competing for awards in extracurricular activities and sports. What if students were to create their own school? What if they had the opportunity to learn what they wanted and the power to choose how they wanted to show their learning?

All students are capable of learning, just not necessarily in the same way or at the same time. We don't expect students to be the best; we hope that they do their best. There is a difference. Our mission as educators is to open the door for students to discover their inner strengths and be aware of their weaknesses, and to know we are there to guide them on their learning journey. We also have to push back our fear of change to do what is best for our students.

Your Fear of Change

Making big changes in the classroom can feel uncomfortable. Any time we try something that might be quite different from what we've been doing, a certain amount of unease might arise, not because there is anything wrong with making changes, but because of the way that many of us experienced school. Traditional methods and practices were followed when we were students, and we still see them being used in classrooms today. When we think back to our own experiences as students, we may recall tests every week, occasional pop quizzes, and nightly homework.

Were you nervous before tests? Were your tests or assignments returned to you covered in red ink? As a student, you might have experienced fear of taking tests, which might have stayed with you throughout your school years. Think back to your experiences and decide what risks you can take to make learning enjoyable and reduce the worry that can come with assessments and learning.

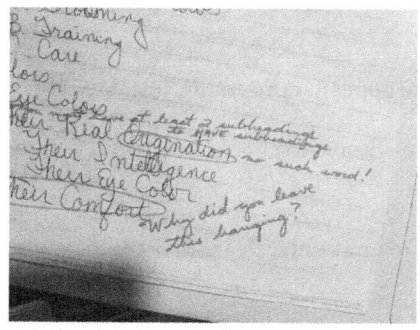

This is why I am not a fan of red ink and carefully choose the feedback that I give.

A Comfortable Space and Pace for Learning

Assessments

The idea of taking an assessment can cause unease in many learners. Even as adults, we often have to take an assessment as part of ongoing professional development, a requirement for administering standardized tests, or possibly proving we have certain skills necessary to carry out a part of our jobs. We have all taken tests and probably have been overwhelmed and nervous, so we can relate to what students feel when it comes to assessments. Perhaps discomfort, like all of the knowledge evaporated when the quiz or project appeared. We must find ways to assess students so they have the confidence to show what they know and can do with the material and are not defeated by worry about the assessment itself.

For educators, the challenge of assessments lies in determining and designing the best format. Our goal is to find out what students know and, more importantly, in a way that will enable all students to feel confident, demonstrating their learning in an authentic way that promotes student choice. Ideally, students should be able to self-evaluate, understand what the data means and how they can take the next steps toward improvement. Thinking about the goals for assessments in schools reminds me of something that Rick Stiggins, author, founder, and president of the Assessment Training Institute stated:

"If you want to appear accountable, test your students;

If you want to improve schools, teach teachers to assess their students;

If you want to maximize learning, teach students to assess themselves."

In traditional assessments, students may receive the same or a similar test or complete the same homework assignments as their classmates. The use of a one-size-fits-all assessment, while it may be more efficient for grading, providing feedback faster and has been traditional for many teachers, it does not fit all of the unique needs and interests of our students. Simply because it helps us to grade faster, does not make it a good assessment. We need to intentionally plan for each of our students.

You can recognize signs of nerves in students. Do any of these sound familiar?

- Students ask for the number of and types of questions.
- Students are curious about how many points the test will be and how many they can miss to keep a certain grade.
- Students ask exactly how to study for it, ask for worksheets, or study guides.
- Students seem to lose all confidence once the test makes its way to their desk, perhaps audibly stating they "don't know anything," or "I am going to fail."

Seeing students shut down and lose confidence so quickly has been something I have become more aware of and trying to find a way to help them defeat their nerves. I've been there and had some bad testing experiences that did not truly show what I knew.

Why do quizzes and tests cause so much worry and a loss in confidence? How can we help students to feel more at ease when it comes to assessments? If only we could eliminate all traditional tests from our classrooms and make room for more student-created assessments and student choice.

Think back to your own experiences and the different assessments that you took. With what types of assessments did you feel more confident and that you were truly able to show your understanding of the content in a way that met your needs? Then think of a time that no matter how hard you studied, you knew the material until the test made its way onto your desk, and then it was as if you had not prepared at all. When I was in law school, I spent months preparing for my final exam in Property Law. I started off strong, but then came to a question that made me lose all confidence, and I struggled to finish. All of that preparation and my knowledge seemed to disappear. Have you experienced something similar? Considering your prior experiences, what would be the most ideal assessment for you?

THERE IS no shortage in ideas of tried and true practices about the best ways to assess students and the frequency of which to do so. There are often debates on the types of assessment being given, if the format is appropriate for measuring learning and whether students should be permitted to retake an assessment in order to improve. Are assessments meant to be a one-time event and the grade received is the grade that stands? If so, what message do we send to students about making mistakes and learning from them to move on?

Students often ask why there have to be so many assessments. Most days, my students are worried about taking a test in one of their classes. What is the effectiveness of tests, which leads students to study and memorize everything, fill in the paper with all of that knowledge, and then move on to the next unit? This was my practice for years, content, quiz, test, repeat. Seeing the impact on students and connecting it with my own experience, I realized there has to be a better way for students to demonstrate mastery of the content. We need to shift the mindset and move away from a focus on points and product, and instead focus on process and growth.

Assessments: Not Just Tests

Depending on the content area and grade level that you teach, there may or may not be specific requirements for the assessments that are used in your classroom. Traditional methods of assessment come in the form of quizzes or tests, projects, or other written or media formats that students create. However, assessments come in many more formats rather than just those which are tangible written or visual products. Students can be assessed in ways that do not even require the creation of anything tangible. By simply having a conversation with teachers or peers, doing a quick check-in, or through simple observations while students complete different activities or tasks in the classroom, students are being assessed. The goal is to grasp the level of understanding that students have and become aware of any difficulties they might be facing.

WHEN STUDENTS PREPARE for traditional forms of assessment such as tests, the manner of learning the material can be somewhat fixed. What this means is that students might prepare for a test by reviewing their notes, class worksheets, and other learning materials that they completed throughout the chapter or unit of study. By doing this, students are preparing for a similar assessment compared to the work they have already done. They prepare by using their materials and anticipate having the exact or a similar format. A low-level application of knowledge. Other times, students may opt to ask their peers what was on the test, the types of questions and the level of difficulty, and will then create their study plan and prepare themselves based on this misinformation. We are obligated to challenge our students to apply knowledge in different ways. One way is to think about the four levels of knowledge outlined in Webb's Depth of Knowledge, a way to categorize levels of complexity developed by Norman Webb (Webb, 2002).

Level 1: (Recall) Students receive information and simply recite facts, low level of complexity, and typically does not require students to expand on the information.

Level 2: (Skill/Concept) Students move beyond simple recall and may participate at a higher level. Common activities are to ask students to classify, compare, interpret, summarize, or organize information.

Level 3: (Strategic Thinking) Students move to a higher level and further explain, expand on topics, apply prior knowledge.

Level 4: (Extended Thinking) Students are applying knowledge in multiple ways, synthesizing information.

Digging Deeper with Webb's DOK

Level 1: *Recall* — Students receive information & simply recite facts, low level of complexity, and typically does not require students to expand on the information.

Level 2: *Skill/Concept* — Students move beyond simple recall & may participate at a higher level. Common activities: classify, compare, interpret, summarize, or organize information.

Level 3: *Strategic Thinking* — Students move to a higher level & further explain, expand on topics, & apply prior information.

Level 4: *Extended Thinking* — Students are applying knowledge in multiple ways, synthesizing information.

@woodard_julie

The four levels focus on a specific result that we want from students.

Do we want students to acquire knowledge (DOK-1) only? Or to acquire and then apply (DOK-2)? Do we want students to analyze (DOK-3) and augment knowledge (DOK-4)? We need to move students beyond simply memorizing content and giving the exact same content back on an assessment or task. Low-level on the DOK is simply a basic recall of information. At this level, students respond to basic facts and questions, knowing the "who, what, where, when, why, and how" of a topic. Recall is memorization and not true attachment to meaning or an extension of learning. It does not enable students to think deeper, explain their thought process, or go beyond "regurgitation" of basic facts. Students will likely not retain the information beyond the short term. They will learn it and then will move on to the next topic. We need to promote learning for life, process over product, and emphasize moving toward mastery. Designing assessments with each student in mind matters because we have to help students understand the benefits of learning for the long-term and not simply to pass a test.

WE NEED to give students more options when it comes to assessments and learning. We know that not every student thrives at taking tests. Again, think of your own experiences. What kind of assessments do you wish that you had?

- Did you get your tests and assignments back covered in red ink? Was there an opportunity for feedback?
- Did you study as much as you could, but not do well because of the test format?
- Were your tests a one-time event without the opportunity to explore your errors and revise so you could keep making progress?

Students likely have more knowledge to share than the test itself can show. Tests that limit students to short answers, multiple-choice, or matching do not allow students to explain their thought processes or show their work, and cannot truly show what students know and can do.

Preparing students for the future requires that we go beyond solely assessing student content knowledge. Regardless of content area or grade level taught, we all need to help students to develop their critical thinking and problem-solving skills while also promoting creativity and curiosity for learning. As teachers, we need to explore different ways of assessing students that will truly show their growth in the content area and help to identify any misunderstandings they have about the material. Teachers need a way to quickly identify students' abilities, and in a way that provides a more personalized and detailed glimpse of where the student is on their learning path. Coming up with alternate forms of assessments can be time-consuming; however, consider strategies that involve students at a deeper level.

"The role of the teacher is to create the conditions for invention rather than provide ready-made knowledge."

SEYMOUR PAPERT, AMERICAN MATHEMATICIAN, COMPUTER SCIENTIST

Strategies for Alternate Assessments

What is your experience with giving tests and offering students the chance to retake them? Is there a way for students to re-assess if their first assessment did not go so well? Retakes were not an option years ago, and as a result of personal experiences, I was led to teach the way I was taught. When it came to tests, students were not able to retake them. For years, my students would ask if there were retakes in my class, and their question was met with a quick "No" without any explanation or time to discuss. My thinking was that sometimes students just lack test-taking skills and need to develop strategies to work through a specific test format. As educators, we need to talk with our students so we can learn about them and be able to offer different options.

Many options are available for assessing students and their level of learning that do not involve the traditional test format, or even the typical project format used as a summative assessment. The key to these alternate assessments is opening up student choice. It means being open to student ideas and taking some risks by letting students determine how to show you what they know and can do with the material. Let them decide their own way to apply it and build on their skills. We simply need to set clear expectations and structure, but then allow students to design their own assessment or demonstration of learning. When we do this, students have a sense of ownership, and they will become more focused on the *process* of learning itself, rather than the end product of a grade or a certain point value. Move away from telling students that the assignment is worth a certain amount of points and instead have checkpoints along the way for students to reach. Once they reach the target, make time for conversations and give students feedback. Assessments do not always need to involve a test or paper. We all have the traditional test formats on hand, so there's not much of a risk in trying one of these methods to see if it makes a difference for students. Take time to get some feedback from the students and to evaluate it yourself to see what the benefits are, what areas could be improved upon, and involve students in the conversation as you move forward.

HERE ARE some ways to promote student choice and voice in learning:

1. **Choose your own assessment**: Why not allow students to create their own assessment? It's understandable that at first, this idea might seem a bit unconventional. You might feel that it would not be in good practice, or might be difficult to maintain, especially with larger classes. But unless you give it a try, you won't know the benefits. It might feel like a risk, but it is worth it, especially when we share with our students that we are trying something different. So why should you present this as an option to students?

The traditional test format can sometimes be a struggle for students. It can feel like they are just memorizing the content to write it back down in the exact same way, or slightly change it to apply to a new situation. Having to keep all of that knowledge fresh only to apply it directly back to the paper does not show what the students have learned or ask them to apply it at a higher level. It might show that they simply prepared well enough before the test and were able to recall information quickly.

Think about the different assessments that you have taken throughout your own educational experiences. Consider these questions:

- Was there a time that you felt all of your knowledge disappeared as soon as you looked at the paper? Simply looking at the test and the questions led you to forget all that you had studied?
- Were there assessments where you were given a choice, but you were unsure about what to create and would have preferred the conventional testing format instead?
- Have you ever allowed students to use their books during a test? I would have never done this years ago, but I have changed my thinking. Depending on the type of test and purpose of the assessment, it might be okay to have students use the book as a resource. We all know that in the real world,

we have instant access to information, and we don't need to rely on the knowledge that we already have or should have.

Taking a test can be a challenge and lead students to experience some anxiety. Providing them with a resource that they can refer to while making connections to their knowledge, can enable them to show what they know while reducing some of the anxiety that the standard test format can cause.

Do an experiment. Rather than giving all students the same test, ask for their ideas, talk about the types of assessments that you have used, and get them involved in giving you some feedback. Explain to them the "why" behind wanting to try the "choose your own assessment" and maybe leave it up to them to decide what to do. Some students may still want to take the traditional test, which is perfectly fine. Other students may prefer to write a story or to create something more authentic and meaningful to show what they have learned throughout the chapter or during a specific unit covered in class. Either way, let students decide what works best for them.

A good way to get started is by setting up some guidelines for you and the students to follow. For example, if students want to create a presentation, regardless of the format, together, you can decide upon a certain number of slides, a specific number of vocabulary terms, or content that they must use in their creation. Trying this for the first time may result in a lot of reflection and changes before proceeding, but at least it involves doing something different that will hopefully and likely attach more meaning to the learning experiences for students so that they are better able to retain the knowledge. Providing students with these types of options is important. It makes learning relevant and establishes a deeper connection with the content. And while it may be unconventional to give students an option to create their own assessments, why not at least give it a try to see how it works out for the students in your classroom. And if you're not ready to go as far as to let students create their own, how about letting students in a class come up with alternatives for sharing their learning. It might come down to having students contribute different types of questions and working together to create an assessment, with your input and additions. The questions would be more reflective of what each student is struggling with in terms of the content and more relevant to their needs. It will be valuable to help students become more self-aware as they select the content they need to work on and will also help students to feel more valued by making the learning decisions in their classroom.

2. **HyperDocs**: Sometimes, it simply takes a visually engaging learning opportunity like a HyperDoc. HyperDocs are digital lesson plans created through Google documents where all components of a lesson have been hyperlinked. HyperDocs are more than a digital worksheet. It is a document with hyperlinks enabling students to work through at their own pace, toward mastery of the goal and acquire the content knowledge that they need. They are powerful, student-driven interactive learning opportunities that offer students an engaging and personalized way to build skills at their own pace and on their own time. They infuse authentic learning because students choose the types of activities and tools and how to show what they have learned throughout the lesson or during a certain part of the course. Creating a HyperDoc does not take much time. To get started, I recommend checking out the *HyperDoc Handbook* by Lisa Highfill, Kelly Hilton, and Sarah Landis. There are also many examples and other resources for using HyperDocs on their website and helpful videos on YouTube.

With HyperDocs, students work through steps of a lesson: Engage, Explore, Explain, Apply, Share, Reflect, and Extend. Be sure to share these steps with students so they can make this part of their learning process. Many examples and explanations of how to get started with HyperDocs can be found on websites. Here are some key things to remember:

- Start with a specific learning target.

- Have a few tools or resources that students can use to get the practice they need, develop their skills, and take advantage of learning any place and at any time.
- Provide students with an overview of how HyperDocs work. The authors of *HyperDoc Handbook* also have helpful videos on YouTube.
- Let students get started, take the time to interact with them and learn from them.

HyperDocs can make a big difference and positively impact student learning. In classrooms where students may not be present for each class meeting, or some students move at different paces, HyperDocs present another way to differentiate instruction. Let's engage students in a new type of learning, where we can enhance what we are already doing in the classroom and allow them to extend their learning in a way that meets their interests and needs. My students enjoyed the change and thought it made learning better because they moved at their pace and they had choices in what they were doing, and what they needed was easily accessible.

3. Conversations and Explorations: A fear of tests is common among students today. Whether the fear comes from prior experiences with tests, or actually comes on as soon as a test is administered, it can lead to students not performing as well as they might be able to, given a different format or testing conditions. Think about how many times you had students come in, and as soon as they receive the test, they proclaim a lack of knowledge or state that they are going to fail or both. It might be common to hear students saying that they knew the answer, they could remember studying it, or they could explain it to you, but all of these comments come after the test has been taken. The test has been given, and the answers are either right or wrong and written, just waiting for the grading to happen.

Teachers have been creating assessments, and students have been taking tests for a very long time. Regular testing has become a natural part of the class routine and in some cases, might be part of a weekly cycle of activities, with students being tested on the same day each week. Teach, practice, test, repeat has become such a conventional method of teaching for many, that it just seems to be a logical progression through each lesson. But it does not have to be this way and it shouldn't.

What if instead, you swap out that test and give students an opportunity to engage in a conversation with you? Have your test ready, but then just make the change on the fly. Share with your students that you are breaking away from the traditional test. Start an open dialogue with your students about the content material. Encourage students to think differently and help them to apply their knowledge in more authentic ways that a standard test cannot show and that gives students more ownership and control.

OR MAYBE TRY SOME "EXPLORATIONS." An exploration would be an opportunity to give students the lead and see where their learning takes them. Provide students with a list of learning targets and the different skills that they need to master. Give them time to explore on their own and develop their own ideas for practice and ways to show their knowledge in a more personalized way. It doesn't always need to involve something tangible like a worksheet or a test. Perhaps simply a conversation between you and them, which promotes more student independence to think about how to show what they have learned.

Of course, with these as well as any other type of assessment, there needs to be time for review and feedback given, as well as a reflection on the effectiveness of these methods. But we won't know what the impact is on students for learning until we push away some of the conventional methods and move into an unconventional and perhaps initially uncomfortable area for us. It is way better to try something and fail than to never try it at all. As teachers, we need to take risks with learning so we can model it for our students.

Reflect

Sometimes when it comes to assessing students, it's not so much about the marks we make on the paper. Without dialogue and involving students in a discussion early, and working with them to set new goals, we will not see their true growth. We must set up a culture for learning—a culture which may be quite different than what we have always done, and likely very different from what we experienced in our own education.

Learning is actively sharing and collaborating. If the only interaction occurring is mostly between the student and the paper, then many wonderful opportunities for learning and growing are missed. Think about how you can change some of the ways you assess in your class-room. They can be minor shifts in what you are already doing, but shifting enough so that students start to feel more comfortable and are excited to let you know what they have learned.

Things to Consider:

1. Take a look at one of your recent assessments. How could you change it into a discussion? Let students talk to you about what they have learned. Forget the paper.
2. Think about the amount of time you spend grading. Do you give written feedback, or are you making time to have conversations with each student? What are some ways you can change your assessment so that the time you spend is engaged in conversation with students rather than confined to writing on the paper?
3. Consider the assessments that you have taken in your lifetime. What are some of the formats that did not help you to truly show your learning? Have you given any of your students the same types of assessments? Can you think of one test that would be better in an alternate assessment format?

#THRIVEinEDU

After reading this chapter, share something that you decided to change in your practice. Feel free to add a photo of the "conventional way" you have assessed students and the unconventional method you are trying now. Use the hashtag #THRIVEinEDU and share!

5 TRANSFORMING LEARNERS TO LEADERS

"The teacher must adopt the role of facilitator not content provider."

LEE S. VYGOTSKY

New Leaders in the Classroom

An English teacher begins working in a prep school where only traditional methods have been used. Students are seen listening to lectures in math and are assigned specific problems to complete for the nightly homework. Every. Single. Day. Enter Mr. Keating, with unorthodox and unconventional methods. He engages students by whistling the 1812 Overture while entering class, taking them on a field trip through the halls of the school, having students remove pages of a textbook that he does not agree with, to demonstrate freedom of expression and non-conformity. His message is that students have the potential to learn and become whatever they want to, the power is within them to determine their future. His motto *Carpe Diem*, Seize the Day, leads students to take actions based on their interests. Students have to learn to think for themselves. His methods are not well received by colleagues, who tell him he cannot get students to be free thinkers at their young age, but it makes him push even harder. He inspired students to question, to learn in new ways, and to develop their voice. In *Dead Poets Society*, the students looked to their teacher as a mentor and a way to go against the traditional ways of learning and to do more than simply consume the content. Keating provided unconventional teaching, and students experienced unconventional, powerful learning.

"The test of a good teacher is not how many questions he can ask his pupils that they will answer readily, but how many questions he inspires them to ask him which he finds it hard to answer."

ALICE WELLINGTON ROLLINS

We Are All Learners

There are so many things that teachers can learn from students. Even though we have traditionally stood in the front of the classroom and have certain qualifications respective to our profession, this does not mean that we are the experts on everything. It certainly does not mean that we have all of the answers to the questions that students might have, contrary to what students tend to think.

Many times, I have been asked questions to which I did not know the answers. As a French and Spanish teacher, it is expected that I know all of the words in the languages that I speak. The reality is that I don't, but wouldn't it be awesome to have those skills? There are tons of words in the English language that I do not know and will not ever learn. As a STEAM teacher, it is expected that I know everything about technology. I do not. Admitting that we do not know the answer to a student question can be uncomfortable, especially in the early years of teaching. But no matter where you are in your career, that fear of not knowing an answer can be difficult to overcome. It can take some time to realize that it's okay to turn to students for answers to questions. In doing this, we are empowering students to be the knowledge seekers and to become curious about learning.

We learn from one another, regardless of our defined "roles" in the conventional classroom. However, if we are only teaching the content that we know and asking questions that we know the answers to, we are limiting the potential growth of our students to our own knowledge levels. We don't do any justice for students preparing for their future nor for ourselves to be able to provide the best and most relevant opportunities for learning. Sometimes an opportunity to get out of the way and let the students lead presents itself, and the choice becomes clear: take a seat in the back and learn from the students. You just go for it. Change your plan on a whim and see what happens. Ask for volunteers to take over the lesson and then decide from there. Do what others might consider to be unconventional. Let the students explore topics to teach you and their classmates. Don't limit the learning to only the material that is covered in the course curriculum and textbook. Be open to those moments that come up inspired by student inquiry and curiosities. Embrace them.

ONE DAY A STUDENT who was against the use of technology for learning decided to create a lesson with Nearpod, a digital tool typically used by teachers. As I started to teach the class that day, this particular student asked if we could do the lesson that he created. As was my habit, I began to lead the lesson myself; however, the student stepped in and said he would like to be the teacher for the day. Initially uncomfortable, and not entirely sure of how it would work out, I decided to just go for it and take the opportunity to experience what it was like to be a student in the classroom. From that moment on, it gave me the idea and the courage to have students take the lead more often.

We Are Better Working Together

Have you ever noticed what happens when someone comes to your classroom? They almost always look to the front and center to find you. The next time someone visits your classroom, see where they look first. Think about your experience teaching and as a student. In your memories, where was the teacher typically found? Even in movies and tv shows about schools, the teacher is typically in the front, standing before rows of students, lecturing from near the chalkboard. But in an unconventional classroom, your initial impression may be that the room is unsupervised because the teacher is not found in that traditional space. You have to look closely until you find the teacher, perhaps in the back of the room, or amongst students at their desks, or even sitting with students at a group of desks and working closely with them. Teachers have made a shift from being the leader to being a co-learner and can be found sitting or standing, learning with and from the students.

Be Okay Moving Aside

For many students in the past as well as today, classrooms have been teacher-centered and/or teacher-focused. If you search for images or videos online, reflect on your own experience as a student, or even think about movies about education you have seen, you might identify with this type of classroom experience. Pretend you are a student and see if this sounds familiar.

> You move by the bell, pass through the hallways, same routine each day.
> You enter the classroom,
> Find and sit in your assigned seat,
> in your assigned row and

wait for the teacher to begin;
You receive instructions about notes to take or activities to do
during class.
You remain active by listening and yet passive while
completing some individual tasks in your seat
until the bell rings, and you move to the next room
and follow the same routine.

If this sounds familiar, that's because many classrooms followed this format, and there are some today that still follow the same classroom setup and routine. Many educators teach as they had been taught, using similar methods and styles of delivering content to students. I did this for many years and realized that there are so many benefits to stepping away from the front of the classroom. It is important to move to the side and instead allow students to do more. To prepare for the future, we need to offer active learning experiences that will promote collaboration, build leadership skills and confidence, and develop communication skills. By shifting away from what may have been a teacher-centered and teacher-driven classroom, we will empower our students to develop their own skills in more authentic and meaningful ways.

Breaking Down the Rows

An unconventional teacher knows that the time has come to break from this traditional structure of classrooms. It is time to break away from students passively learning and not having opportunities to truly engage in activities within the classroom, to be the ones asking the questions and leading the lesson. They should have time to be social in learning by interacting with peers. They need opportunities to design their own learning paths in order to be best prepared for whatever the future brings. Giving students more of an opportunity to control the pace and the type of learning that occurs in the class-room will create a more meaningful attachment and investment in learning. Changing our roles by stepping back and becoming facilitators of learning, rather than the leaders, will empower students to develop their advocacy and leadership skills. We must actively seek ways for students to do more than passively interact with the content in the classroom. When we provide encouragement for students and scaffold opportunities for them to be the creators, become more active, and collaborate with peers, it fosters student agency, builds student comfort and confidence as they evolve into leaders.

WITH STUDENTS MAKING MORE decisions in the classroom, by choosing their learning path, and creating lessons to share with classmates, they will develop many of the critical future ready skills of collaboration, problem-solving, critical thinking, and communication. Students become the new classroom leaders, which enables teachers to step into the role of facilitator and use the extra class time to instead move around the classroom, learn more about the students and their needs, personalize the learning experience for students, and build relationships in the process. We can take time to sit and learn with and from them and share their work within our school. When we create new opportunities for students to step up and lead, we promote student choice and build confidence, empowering students to drive their learning. We create a unique learning experience for our students in a space that they can learn in and lead from. We must DARE to be different in our classrooms: Dream, Advocate, Risk, and Empower!

A Plan to Know and Grow

Many people, whether involved in education or not, remember and maybe even have strong memories of their own experiences in the classroom. Chances are, some of the experiences would be the same for many students regardless of when and where they went to elementary school and high school. Recalling the structure of class-rooms, the routines for each class, and what students did during each class period, may uncover very similar recollections of the look and feel of school. Asking adults to share some of their best learning moments would be a good way to start some conversations. Perhaps create a poll to gather some feedback and focused on a few questions such as:

- How often did students make the decisions about how to share their learning with their audience, whether it be classmates, other classrooms in the school, or even branching out into the community?
- Did you have a choice, or were you simply told what to do?
- What similar methods are you using with your own students today?

Our past experiences always give us something to think about for our future. Use these experiences, both good and bad, to help guide you as you make decisions for your own students. Connect students with real-world learning opportunities and break away from the conventional methods and learning tools that were used by your own teachers. Students need chances to speak, to lead, and to create. It's time to move out of the way and let them lead.

SOME STRATEGIES CAN LEAD to incredible opportunities for students and teachers, which foster curiosity for learning and increase student engagement. The variety of learning concepts and different perspectives that have come into the classroom as a result of doing these activities has provided far more information, insight, and cultural awareness than one teacher standing alone in the front of the room possibly could. Even with all of the online resources available such as videos and other media and text, the power of learning multiplies greatly when we recognize that everyone in the classroom has something to teach. If we open these opportunities to our students and have them do more of the talking rather than us, their learning will be much greater and of course, more authentic and meaningful.

Think about the following:

- Do you lead discussions and ask all of the questions in class?
- Do students have opportunities to take the lead?
- Do students have opportunities to collaborate with peers often?
- What can we do to build student confidence, leadership skills, and increase engagement in learning?

Stepping aside creates a fantastic way to give students more control in the discussion and to spark their curiosity for learning. Experiences like this make it relevant and meaningful to each individual student and for the class as a whole. There are many ways we can encourage students to take more of a lead, but it depends on the group of students and their individual needs. We may have students in our classroom who are quite shy or do not want to speak up in front of their peers. Many adults in their roles as educators, at times, struggle with the same thing that they might ask students to do. For years I did not understand why students did not want to speak in front of their peers, yet when I was placed in the same position to speak in front of mine, I avoided it as much as I could. It was uncomfortable.

In order to provide some level of comfort, perhaps start by having students work with one peer. Sometimes working with a classmate helps students to build confidence before leading the whole class or even just small groups. Starting with a small activity and then building up, can definitely help students to gain the confidence that they need before trying one of these "leadership" type activities. Some strategies for increasing student involvement and shifting your role to that of a learner are Teacher for a Day, Project-based learning, Genius Hour, Ted-ED club activities, and Student-led PD.

1. Teacher for a Day

A good strategy for helping students to make the shift from learner to leader and develop confidence is to design a "Teacher for a Day" activity. Start by thinking about content that you cover that might be challenging for students or perhaps you need new instructional ideas for. Is there a topic that you would like to expand upon? Use your curiosity for learning as a starting point for students. Bring the students in and give them the chance to create a new way of learning. Decide on specific themes or maybe instead leave it to the students and have them design a lesson to teach to their peers. At first, some students might feel uncomfortable about this unconventional practice because they will be designing and delivering the lesson, rather than simply turning in a project or an assignment to their teacher. However, the comfort will come from knowing that they have control over determining the content and format of their lesson. Creativity will definitely be promoted in this "Teacher for a Day" activity, and it will be a more meaningful experience for everyone.

Once they have created a lesson, you should then trade places with the student. By having your "Teacher for a Day" lead the lesson, give explanations, ask and answer questions, it will create a more engaging learning opportunity for all "learners" in the classroom, including you. When students ask a question and look to you for the answer, you can then direct the question to the Teacher for the Day. In my own classroom, this was something that the students really enjoyed doing because they made the decisions and had more ways to share ideas and show learning. Activities like this create a lot of opportunities for students to think critically and problem solve, and continue to build their collaborative nature and interpersonal skills.

Students who have participated in this have enjoyed being the teacher, having a new way to practice, collaborate, and provide good feedback to their classmates. It is very rewarding to see students develop their leadership skills and confidence as they transform from learners to leaders. Being able to co-design learning experiences will challenge students to think beyond simply what the content itself is, but brainstorm ideas together on the best ways to master the content and in ways which are purposeful and unique to them. Perhaps even trying student-led Edcamps, where multiple students take the lead within small groups, similar to the Edcamps that many educators have attended.

2. PBL

Project-Based Learning (PBL) is a unique way to learn from the students and focus on the process of learning rather than the product. It is a beneficial way to promote student-driven inquiry, where students craft their own driving or essential question and explore something that is of personal interest or a passion for them. PBL promotes critical thinking, creativity, and problem-solving, and serves to amplify the learning potential for every student as they begin to design their own learning path. Through PBL, students can communicate and collaborate globally, bringing in real-world examples and relevant information to build their project-based learning experience. In addition to promoting student choice and student agency through self-directed learning, doing PBL provides an opportunity to learn more about the students and their interests, to become a co-learner with them, and shift to a facilitator of learning rather than being the only teacher in the room. By shifting roles, we also expand the content that is covered in class, which leads to more engaged students, driven by curiosity in a student-led environment.

But It Takes Too Much Time

Many educators might find Project-Based Learning (PBL) challenging to start. However, many resources are available, and it simply takes jumping right in with the students to learn together. Some PBL resources include *Hacking PBL* by Ross Cooper and Erin Murphy (2017), *Project Based Teaching: How to Create Rigorous and Engaging Learning Experiences* by Suzie Boss with John Larmer (2018), and blogs by educators like John Spencer and A.J. Juliani. I also recommend PBL Works from the Buck Institute of Education, which provides samples, rubrics, the essential elements of PBL, and much more.

Why PBL? We need to create opportunities for students to dig deeper into learning and pursue something that is of interest to them, and that will promote ongoing exploration and curiosity. The most difficult part for students is often thinking about how to present their information. Students have become used to completing projects, typically at the end of a unit of learning, so they are focused on one end product. But if you focus on the end product first, it will limit possible learning opportunities or prevent students from discovering new information that would prove beneficial to their learning. Being able to make their own decisions with such independence, for some, is unconventional. However, opportunities like this which enable students to become more independent and have choices for where their search leads, amplify the learning potential of all students in the classroom.

3. Genius Hour

You don't need to teach in a specific content area to try Genius Hour. You just need a little bit of information to get started in your classroom. What are the benefits of using Genius Hour with your students? Through activities such as this, we help students to develop their voice and leadership skills. As educators, we can create new and more engaging opportunities for our students to explore their passions and become more connected with the content that they are learning. In the process, we will better understand who our students are and what they are passionate about.

Genius Hour is a meaningful opportunity for students to engage in inquiry-based and student-driven learning. Teachers can promote student choice and foster student agency by providing time for students to explore their interests. Sometimes Genius Hour has been referred to as 20% time, whereas the remaining 80% is the traditional classroom instruction, and the 20% is the unconventional time set aside for students. For 20% time, students have time in class to work independently and come up with ideas for how they will share their knowledge and have the opportunity to teach their peers as well as their teacher.

Genius Hour has many benefits. It promotes student curiosity, encourages collaboration, helps to develop social skills, and increases student confidence and comfort. Genius Hour offers students a chance to share something that they know about, they are passionate about, in a learning environment where student choice is promoted. The approach puts students in the lead. What's even better is that your students will be talking about Genius Hour in their other classes and with their peers, so it's an idea that can definitely spread and encourage other teachers to give it a try.

To get started with Genius Hour, I recommend *Pure Genius* by Don Wettrick (2017) for ideas and inspiration. Don created an Innovation Class at his school, and he encourages starting with clear guidelines. Take time to talk about Genius Hour with your students, get their feedback, and then set up a plan to get started.

To begin, have students:

1. Select a topic
2. Determine an essential or driving question.
3. Plan the 20% time in your class schedule.
4. Facilitate student inquiry, only stepping in when needed.
5. Prepare for the student presentations.
6. Ask for and offer feedback.

Of course, as with any innovation, it may take a little time to get Genius Hour set up, but that's just another way to reinforce that learning is a process, and it's not about the product. Genius Hour is about allowing students to share whatever their genius might be. Maybe it's music, sports, cooking, or any of their passions. Shining the light on each student is an excellent way to build connections and add to the classroom culture. Follow Don's motto, "There is no plan. Success comes when you learn to adapt and innovate" (Pure Genius, p. 29). I also recommend checking into Don's STARTedUP Foundation and podcast to hear from some student innovators.

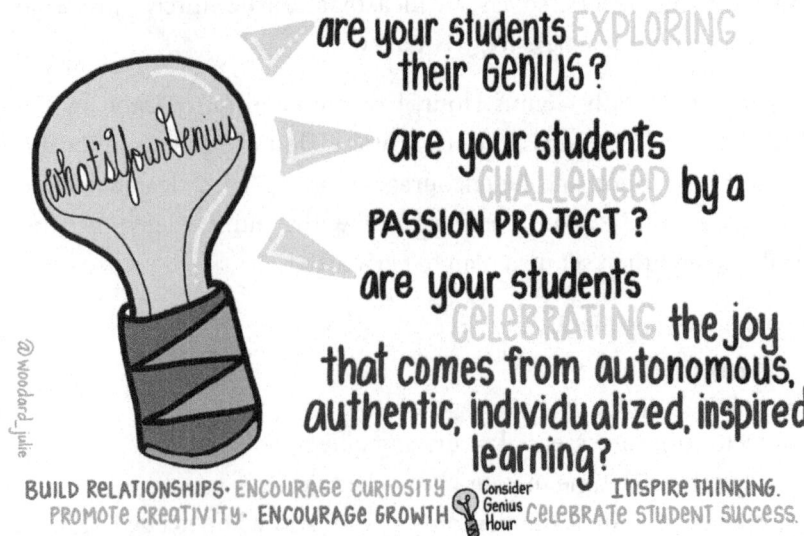

are your students EXPLORING their GENIUS?

are your students CHALLENGED by a PASSION PROJECT?

are your students CELEBRATING the joy that comes from autonomous, authentic, individualized, inspired learning?

BUILD RELATIONSHIPS· ENCOURAGE CURIOSITY   Consider   INSPIRE THINKING.
PROMOTE CREATIVITY· ENCOURAGE GROWTH   Genius Hour   CELEBRATE STUDENT SUCCESS.

4. TED-Ed: Rising to the Challenge

Initiating a TED-Ed club is another effective way to build student confidence and to let students explore their passions. While many schools may offer courses focused on public speaking, or students can join school organizations that help them to develop leadership skills, not all students have these opportunities. Some simply cannot fit them into their schedule, and others may fear being involved and putting oneself out there in front of a larger group, especially when the group is their peers. But an interesting transformation happens when the topic focuses on a student's passion and experience. Through the process of sharing their knowledge, they gain confidence.

Applying to start one of the TED-Ed clubs presents an opportunity to empower students to become leaders in the classroom today as well as the leaders of tomorrow. The idea comes from TED talks, and as part of the TED-Ed clubs, students work through an idea book full of "explorations" that help them to identify their passions or find something that they are curious about. There are no limits to what students can decide to explore for their passion project. The goal is to share an "idea worth spreading." Working through the resources provided through TED-Ed can help students to develop future ready skills in addition to those of confidence, collaboration, and leadership. Becoming part of the club brings diverse students together who can create their own learning community and build social-emotional learning skills as they work with their peers and develop an under-standing of the differences as well as the commonalities between them. It builds culture and global awareness when students can invest in meaningful exploration of their passions and become independent thinkers, driven by their curiosity for learning.

Find your VOICE, so students find THEIRS.

Finding Our Voices

If you have students who tend to be shy in class, but when given the right space (virtual or physical), they find their voice, encourage them to become a member of TED-Ed. Sometimes students might be hesitant to join such clubs because the thought of speaking in front of others might be overwhelming. We know that public speaking is one of the greatest fears for many people, and our students might need some preparation before feeling comfortable speaking in front of the group. Planning introductory activities to connect students with one another and building their confidence together leads to a positive outcome.

When students take the opportunity to stand up and share their passions, the potential for learning and sharing of knowledge goes far beyond the individual student and the teacher. We can share their work publicly, and in the school community, teachers will see students in a new light and better understand their interests, which will further strengthen the building of relationships. Our goals are to inspire students to share their stories, promote growth mindset, and reinforce the idea of learning as a process and not for a product. It sends the message that everyone has a voice and needs to be heard. Although there is a designated teacher in the classroom, students have as much to offer when it comes to learning. We all have something to teach and something to learn. We are definitely better together.

5. Student-Led Professional Development

As teachers, we may spend most of our time as a leader, not a learner. Opportunities for teachers to continue on their lifelong learning path either occur during school district scheduled professional development days or as part of a teacher's personalized professional development plan. One of the benefits of having teachers together in PD sessions is time to collaborate with colleagues, whereas finding time for this regularly can be difficult. Teachers are doing many great things in classrooms every day, but many of these ideas stem from the innovative ideas of students. We can learn much from our students, and we need to be intentional about sharing these stories, so we can empower others. While teachers can lead PD sessions and share what is happening in their classroom, why not use the time to have the students speak to teachers about their experiences instead. Hearing directly from students will be beneficial and create a connection between teachers and students.

A common criticism of traditional PD is that it is not personalized enough for what teachers need. Imagine how powerful it would be to have students lead the way. Sharing what they are doing in the classroom and what helps them to learn best can be a powerful session of learning for everyone. Creating an opportunity for students to provide feedback to teachers about what strategies and tools help them to learn best, and add their different ideas into the classroom, will help students to feel more valued in the classroom and create a more meaningful experience. Invite students to share their projects, so that teachers can see the work being done in other courses. When students share their work, teachers can better understand students' unique interests and needs and gather some new ideas about ways to engage students in their classes. If we want our students to experience personalized learning and share what they do, then we should invite students to become the leaders and deliver full professional development sessions in our school.

Last spring, several of my students presented multiple PD sessions discussing their tech tips, tools, and tricks, teaching their teachers about how to use different digital tools. It was the first time this was done, and it created a more personalized way for teachers to learn from students and to understand directly how different strategies and digital tools can make a difference in the learning potential for students.

Your Plan to Step Aside

Although as educators, we typically stand in the classroom and deliver the instruction, we are not necessarily the experts. It is simply that we have more experience in what we are doing. We are constantly learning and should actively seek new ways to bring knowledge and create learning experiences for our students. We need to think about unconventional ways to involve students more in lesson design and classroom strategies and to start by stepping aside and letting them lead the way.

Ask: Invite feedback from your students after their "Teacher for a Day" experience. Think back on your own experience as a student in your classroom. Did you learn any new strategies from your students? I would bet that you did, as I know that I have gotten many ideas from my students. They always have some really creative ideas!

Reflect

After trying one or all of these activities in your classroom, set aside some time to have follow-up conversations with your students and ask them for honest feedback. It is amazing how open the students can be when we set the right conditions by forming a trusting relationship where they feel free to share their ideas. Consider the following:

- What was the impact on student learning by being the Teacher for a Day?
- What did you learn about your students by switching roles in the classroom?
- How can this experience help you to better prepare for your students?
- What was the student's response to being in control of the lesson, deciding how to teach, and leading their classmates through the class?

By giving the students a chance to not only absorb but to create, design, and think critically, we help them to develop the knowledge to be successful. We encourage them to create their own path to success, and hopefully, in the process, they learn to better self-assess and reflect and emerge as confident leaders.

1. Step aside: Be okay with letting the students take over. Sometimes the greatest learning happens in the most unconventional ways.
2. Explore: Design your own PBL or apply to create your own TED-Ed club and learn right along with the students.
3. Ask: Seek input from students on the activities they want to do in class.

#THRIVEinEDU

Now is your chance to share which of these ideas you tried in your classroom or in your school. What are some of the most noticeable changes, or what was the impact of implementing a Teacher for a Day or implementing project-based learning? Share your experience by blogging and tweet it out using the hashtag #THRIVEinEDU.

6 IGNITING A PASSION FOR KNOWLEDGE

"Provide an uncommon experience for your students and they will reward you with an uncommon effort and attitude."

DAVE BURGESS, AUTHOR, TEACH LIKE A PIRATE

For four seasons in the 1970s, the TV show *Welcome Back Kotter* brought a lot of laughs and insights about life and high schools to American households. This show was based on the classroom of Gabe Kotter, a fictional teacher portrayed by Gabe Kaplan, in charge of "controlling" a class full of diverse and disruptive students, many needing remediation and not too interested in being students. The "Sweathogs," a group of students led by Vinnie (John Travolta), caused classroom mishaps, had incomplete homework assignments, experienced personal struggles, exhibited many unique, quirky and challenging learning styles, and sometimes even dealt with serious societal issues that were addressed in the show. What made the show stand out and grab your attention is that Mr. Kotter did not let everyone else's opinion of these students (not even the students' opinions of themselves) diminish his passion for teaching and lifting them up. He formed a relationship with each of them, found ways to connect on a personal and truly authentic level, and inspired them to pursue their dreams, even when other teachers, administrators, or they themselves thought they were incapable of being successful in life.

The message from the show is that teachers are obligated to truly know their students, understand their passions, help them to learn from mistakes, and not tell them what to do, but also to be there to help them when they fall. Mr. Kotter was not the only teacher in the classroom. Each "Sweathog" developed into a leader, pursuing acts of charity, developing empathy, and paying it forward. Besides teaching the content, Gabe taught students lessons of life and worked beyond the school day to help them pursue their passions. Regardless of their success or failure, he did not give up on them. He provided the "Sweathogs" with unconventional opportunities to learn that met their interests, rather than simply covering the curriculum. Arranging trips, helping them to plan fundraisers, and getting them started in a new direction inspired each student to push themselves to do more and prove that they were capable of much more than others, or even they expected. Although the show was fictional, the message is relevant and clear today. Educators need to embrace the specific needs and interests of students and help them to overcome challenges faced in the pursuit of their own dreams.

"Be diligent in trusting that what we do today in the classroom could possibly echo for a lifetime in the heart of a student."

ROBERT JOHN MEEHAN, AMERICAN EDUCATOR

Student Interests and Passions for Learning

Every student traditionally does their own project, and, in many cases, only the teacher sees it, and then the work is returned to the student and likely discarded. Why? Why not have the class do collaborative presentations? Focus on students sharing as they learn together, building more than just content skills, but also working on social-emotional learning skills, collaboration, and communication. Projects and learning don't have to be over and done. Student work can become next year's new resources for students. How can we take what the students create and use it for enrichment and as our instructional materials for years to come? We build an active, student-driven class-room, with opportunities for authentic work and for students to contribute to the classroom design.

STUDENTS SPEND a lot of time in the classroom, and most of that time is spent sitting and listening. Between the years of kindergarten through 12th grade, students spend an average of 11,700 hours in a classroom setting (Sheninger & Murray, 2017 p. 115). Depending on the school structure and the way that a particular school's scheduling works, the time spent can vary from classes that meet every day with maybe a 40- or 50-minute period, or slightly longer, to a few days per week if schools are operating on a block schedule. Another important factor of this "equation" is the number of students enrolled in each class. Figure out, on average, how much time would be available for each student to interact with their teachers daily. The likelihood is that there would not be much time per student. For example, in my school, our class periods are forty-two minutes. If I have an average class size of twenty-one students and do not use any time standing in front of the room teaching, then each student has at most two minutes for interacting with me each day. After meeting five days, if this were a typical class routine, ten minutes of my time would be spent per student per week. Is this enough time for our students to be successful and to feel supported? Maybe, if other methods are in place for students to interact and receive support from their teacher.

Making Time for Connecting

The more time we spend with each student, the greater the impact we make on their learning and social-emotional skills. Personally, I'm torn between deciding if I would prefer to have at least one interaction every single day, or would the benefits be greater by having ten minutes to sit down and actually have a longer, more focused conversation with each student once a week? What would yield better results? What if we took one class period per week and had students explore something on their own? If students could make choices about their learning path and have time to explore, it would create more time for individual conversations, if just for a quick check in with each student. Finding time to learn about them and their passions is critical, but do we take away from time spent on the content?

WOULD THERE BE a big sacrifice of the amount of content covered over the school year if using one class period for students to explore their interests was to become a regular classroom practice? Doing quick math based on a typical schedule, roughly thirty-six class periods (40 minutes each) would be removed from the 180-day school year and replaced by time for interacting with each student. Every opportunity for teachers to speak with the students, even if it is only a quick conversation as they're entering or leaving the classroom, will strengthen these relationships. The more that teachers learn about students, the better it is for the classroom environment and students' learning experience. Building connections can boost students' learning because they will feel valued and connected to one another in the classroom.

There is no substitute for having the time to sit and talk with students, to really get to know what they are bringing to the class-room, as well as their background, experiences, interests, abilities, and feelings about the class. However, there are ways that teachers can infuse activities to get a better picture of each student and figure out ways to more meaningfully connect the content with student inter-ests. These are only temporary substitutes for those conversations but will help with building up relationships and promoting a positive classroom culture.

Sometimes when students are asked about their interests, they may not feel comfortable responding or sometimes just don't really know what to say. An ice breaker to do at the start of the year (or any time) that works well involves a simple Google survey (that does not even require students to enter their name). A wide variety of questions can be asked. While the students take the survey, the teacher has an opportunity to move around the classroom and have side conversa-tions. One thing to listen for is when students read the questions aloud and openly state that they're "not sure what to write," or they "don't have any idea," or ask for clarification on some questions. In my experience, two of the most common questions that students struggle with answering are: What is something unique about you, and what are three words that you would use to describe yourself? In every class that took my survey, these were the questions that students struggled with the most. Several students said they didn't know what to say about themselves because they didn't want it to come across as though they were bragging. Other students said there wasn't anything unique or different about them, and that they were just like everybody else. A few students responded, "I don't know" or simply wrote the word "nothing," which led me to think about how I could encourage students to share more of who they are. Knowing how to respond to some of their answers doesn't always come easily; however, the best advice that I have offered to students is to think about how a friend might describe them if asked.

Here are some prompts:

- Tell students to imagine that a friend was asked to describe them by naming three facts, sharing a funny memory, or naming a personality trait. What might they say?
- Encourage the student to think of how others have described them in the past. Everyone has a way they are thought of by others.
- Ask students to share an athletic ability, favorite activity, a skill, or random fun facts. This slight push might just help to break the ice and encourage students to express who they are and what passions they have.

A Way for Students to Lead

How many times have you had students say that they didn't know what they were interested in, didn't want to participate in an activity, or didn't like something? If we were to gather 50 people into a room and ask them to compare their current profession with what they thought they might do when they were in high school or somewhere in between, I wonder how many people are doing what they imagined? How many people might actually be shocked at where they ended up on their learning journey through life? I know that I would, and can think of several friends and family members that would feel the same.

❊

As a French student in high school and college, I didn't really think about going into education. Even when I did enter the profession, I thought that I might only work as a teacher for about ten years. Not that I had plans for what I would do after that time, it just seemed to be enough time to spend in a career before moving on to something else.

For students, one of the main purposes of school is to expose them to different learning opportunities and experiences. We want them to pursue electives and make choices in their learning. Even when students might push back about trying something different, we must encourage them to at least give it a go before deciding that they are not interested. Sharing our stories about how we explored things along our way, and how we got to where we are today, can help students as they navigate their own way.

Some highly-motivated students may have personal areas of interest or are passionate about a certain subject. Knowing this can help us to channel their motivation as a way to encourage their peers toward exploring their passions in school. It's important to give students these opportunities so that later on in life, when challenges arise or if they decide to go in a different direction, they have background experiences that they can draw from to move ahead. Many strategies can help students find out what their passions are. Some of these strategies can be used with the whole class or set up for each individual student.

Depending on the course and the grade-level taught, the applicability and benefit of each of these strategies can vary, but the underlying purpose, the "why" behind each of them, is still the same. We want to promote student choice and voice, to spark curiosity for learning, to encourage students to explore, create, reflect, and develop a broader understanding of how the world works and the opportunities available. And what is even better than students uncovering their own interests and passions, is when they can share their knowledge and the products they create with their peers. We all benefit because we have new resources available for current as well as future students. It is also a talking point when students may be uncomfortable exploring on their own, they can start a conversation with their peers, and sometimes that is just the motivation and confidence booster needed to get them started and to build that initial level of comfort.

As EDUCATORS, we can try many strategies to provide support for our students and encourage them to get started in a new direction. But the power of peer collaboration is even greater. When students develop their own PLN, which can be a "peer learning network," students will become comfortable stepping in to help whenever their peers need it. Building comfort and confidence and fostering those relationships will engage students in the classroom. We promote student choice and voice in learning by providing opportunities for students to become the creators and share what they create with their peers as well as future students.

1) Class Collaboration: One way to find out about student interests is to give them an opportunity to collaborate in a Google Document, Google Slides presentation, or Microsoft PowerPoint. It might even be some-thing like collaborating on a Padlet, where students can share interests and ideas or come up with solutions to problems together. When students work together like this, they not only build their collaborative skills, but they also develop their social-emotional learning skills, which are vital for student growth. These collaborative adventures can help students to become self-aware, learn to express themselves, and develop knowledge about real-world issues. Learning matters. When students take the initiative and drive their own learning, all we need to do is to give them a starting point and let them explore and create on their own.

Think about whether or not you want to have the entire class working on the same presentation. For example, if trying this for the first time, you want to make sure to set some guidelines about respecting the work of others. Opportunities like this are beneficial for many reasons, an important one of which includes continuing to build the digital citizenship skills of our students. Because these tools promote real-time collaboration, it is easy to intentionally or accidentally change the work of another collaborator. Thus, it is a good idea to have a conversation about the value of respecting the work of others, of being responsible when creating, and of keeping focused on the positive value in the power of these tools for promoting learning within one classroom or connecting globally.

Here are a few ways to get started with a "Class Collaboration."

- At the beginning of the year, create a presentation where students can add one slide of information about themselves.
- Provide one slide with instructions or an "About Me" theme.
- Provide each student with access to the presentation and give some time for students to create one slide to introduce themselves.
- Before displaying the whole presentation in class, check to make sure all students have completed their task, and all slides are appropriate.
- Use the slides as discussion starters and for students to make connections with one another.

Doing an activity like this is a comfortable way for students to learn about their classmates. They will discover interesting or little-known facts that they have in common, which helps to lay the foundation for building vital relationships.

The "class collaboration" idea can be used with project-based learning. Gather all of the student topics into one presentation and ask each student to add one slide to serve as an advertisement for their topic and essential question. Maybe ask students to use minimum text and a few images to grab the attention of their peers, which can generate interest and spark curiosity.

Throughout the year, many types of projects can be done using this same format. We can branch out to do cross-curricular projects or multi-level collaborative projects, such as in language classes, having students in different levels of language classes, or even grade levels, collaborate on one presentation. Students can work in small teams on one presentation, with each student having an assigned role or task. Encourage them to discuss their roles and set expectations for respecting one another's work. Let the students plan their work and tasks and learn to self-regulate in the process. In the end, besides the more authentic and meaningful learning that takes place, we create an environment that fosters strong peer relationships, which can be challenging to form in the traditional classroom space.

Comfort grows

By starting these collaborations in the online space, the comfort with interactions will transfer to the physical space. Sometimes this is what has worked the best to help my students build connections with their peers. Students can feel awkward joining with a new group in class or working with peers whom they don't know well. But when we add in fun and possibly unconventional ways to collaborate, we can create more excitement for learning. We are not only promoting student voice and choice, but we are also showing students that learning can happen anywhere.

Another helpful option is an interactive review presentation. Rather than creating a review packet *for* students, allow students to create their own review materials for the class. Each student can select from class topics and add in activities and resources to enrich the content material, which personalizes the learning experience for all students. This collaboration also encourages students to help where they have strengths in the material to work with their peers. When my own students have done this collaborative presentation, it has become a great review resource for other classes in later years.

2. **Student-Led Edcamps:** Have you ever been to an Edcamp? For most people, the first time attending an Edcamp can be confusing. Edcamps are unlike traditional professional development sessions or conferences where the schedule and topics are pre-determined, and you kind of go through and move when you need to move, and typically do not have many choices. At an Edcamp, defined sessions or schedules are not prepared in advance. The attendees decide the topics to be included upon arrival. Talk about choices in learning! Take the same concept and try running a student-led Edcamp in one of your classes or all of your classes. It's quite easy to do.

- Distribute post-it notes to each student.
- Explain the concept of an Edcamp and how you will use it in class.
- Ask students to write topics or specific content that they might need some help with and add topics where they feel they could explain a strategy, a tech tool, or an idea to someone else.
- Next, begin to organize the Post-it notes by similar topics to determine five or six focus areas.
- Create a "board" or a schedule of student-facilitated sessions for the class period.
- Designate spaces in your room for students to gather for each of the sessions.

Trying Edcamps in the classroom is a good way to put students in the lead and offer opportunities to keep on collaborating and building relationships.

How does it look in the classroom? For example, if you teach an English course and students are reading a novel, their questions or strengths might fall into categories related to the vocabulary used, the theme, the character analysis, or questions in general about the style of the book. Students can write down whatever it is they need help with or would like to help others with, and by creating these sessions, students have the choice to learn from or lead their peers in areas where they feel most comfortable. Divide it up so that perhaps during one class period, students may choose two of the sessions and then allow time for the class to provide feedback. The idea is to give students a chance to all lead in the conversation and share whatever it is they want to, either questions about or experience with the topic or strategies for how to better understand it.

The best part is giving students the chance to design the lesson and methods for learning by making their own space in the classroom. It enables you to get a better idea of areas that students need help with and creates extra time to move around and interact with each group and work on those relationships.

3. **Leave it to them!** Have you ever prepared an activity for class (i.e., a worksheet, something hands-on, a video, or maybe a game), but then decided right before starting that you didn't really like that plan at all? Or you had something lined up, that required technology, and it failed? For whatever reason, you have to make changes at the last minute and go in a different direction. Many times, I grab that worksheet and start to pass it out, then decide that I wouldn't even want to do it! In times like this, why not involve students and leave it to them to decide.

Not having a plan and leaving it up to the students might sound scary. It can be! But if you've never done this, then how can you really know? Of course, it involves a little bit of a risk, but when we spend time building relationships in our classroom and students know that we value their input, it's more likely that they will enjoy the opportunity to come up with innovative ways to practice. And if it helps, maybe ask students for some suggestions, write the list on the board, and then let students choose. You can move around and facilitate, but give students the chance to drive their own learning for the day and see where it leads them and you. There's always room to improve, and this might be the first step on a new path to more meaningful, student-driven learning.

By giving students more voice in the classroom and an opportunity to do something different than simply learn the planned curriculum and content, but rather explore new areas and learn about themselves, we open a world full of opportunities for all learners. Sometimes it requires teachers to use unconventional teaching methods and step out of comfort zones, but the end result is more student agency and empowerment in learning.

> Teachers need to stop saying, "Hand it in," and start saying "Publish It."
>
> **ALAN NOVEMBER**

New Methods

We are all learners, and one of the best ways to create an interactive and collaborative learning experience is by promoting active student learning and leading. It might be uncomfortable for teachers at first to give up some control, and for some students to think about leading in a small group or working with peers, they may not have worked with before. By starting slowly and then adding on each of these activities, we can build the confidence of every student.

Get started by facilitating those online interactions by using a Google Doc or Microsoft PowerPoint where students can work together, build a relationship, and be more social with learning but in that safe virtual learning space. Their comfort will transfer over into the physical classroom. You can then continue to build student confidence further by moving to the Edcamp activity and then give them more voice by having them determine the lesson for the day.

Reflect

It can be uncomfortable to do less of the planning and leave more up to your students. Think about the impact it has when you have been given more choices in your own professional learning. Identify some of the content you cover and the different methods you've used that may not have been effective for all students. We know there is not a one-size-fits-all method. Imagine allowing the students to design their own learning pathways. How would you feel if given a chance to design your own professional development and be able to share your learning with colleagues? The benefits would be tremendous. If you are already participating in professional development like this, then you know what a difference it makes. Let's provide this for our students too.

TAKE a step today and choose one of these to get started right now. Set aside time to roll it out in class and then ask for student feedback before moving on to another idea.

1. Create a collaborative project for all students to participate in. Give them a slide to follow with the instructions and have them work on it in class so you can assist during the first time. Make time for feedback and then try it again.
2. Grab some Post-it notes, create a space on your board or wall, and give students the opportunity to create their own learning sessions. Have a few students help you organize the responses, set up the "board," and then get started with your official

student-led Edcamp. Be sure to join the sessions as well just to learn from the students.

3. Step aside for the day and give students one goal: Come up with a way to practice the content or specific topic for the class period. Let them determine how to spend their time and use your time to move around and learn from their ideas. Be sure to interact with them often and to facilitate a whole-class conversation later to get some ideas for the next time.

#THRIVEinEDU

Share your ideas for placing students in the lead and how your first collaborative presentation went. Were there any issues that helped to reinforce digital citizenship? Post some pictures of your official Edcamp board or even share some of the ways the students chose to practice when they led for the day. Share it out with the hashtag #THRIVEinEDU.

"Be creative. Use unconventional thinking. And have the guts to carry it out."

LEE IACOCCA, AMERICAN EXECUTIVE

BE creative.
USE unconventional THINKING.
and HAVE the GUTS to CARRY it OUT

Dladenb

7 TECHNIFYING THE LEARNING ADVENTURES

[Quoted from Bill Gates, image by Monica Spillman]

People often talk about today's classrooms and make comparisons with the way they looked years ago, when there was very little technology, and teaching methods were quite different. In most schools today, the amount of technology available to teachers and students is tremendous. For some, it can be overwhelming to get started with tech, but the benefits can be significant for learning. We have the power to learn almost anything, anywhere, at any time. Teachers and students do not even have to be in the same physical learning space anymore. What power in being able to learn at a time and place that is convenient and possibly even more comfortable!

One aspect that technology truly helps with is eliminating a definitive break in opportunities for learning. How many times did the bell ring before teachers and students could finish their thoughts? Once class ended, students typically did not have access to teacher support or resources beyond the school day. Now, if students are completing an assignment or working on a project at home, whether in the evening or over the weekend, they can send messages or access materials whenever they need to. Technology leveraged for this purpose is powerful.

THERE WILL ALWAYS BE pushback when it comes to the integration of technology in the classroom, but the truth is that technology has opened many doors to new opportunities in education and in life. Not that technology is the answer or should just be used for the sake of using it, but regardless of what you teach, we all share in the responsibility to help our students develop the right skills and learn to use technology responsibly. We now live in a highly digital and connected world, and our students aged 13-18 spend, on average, nine hours every day using their phones for purposes besides learning. Knowing this, we should embrace the technology, and meaningfully connect the devices to what we are teaching. By intentionally planning how to weave the technology into our classrooms, we can help students to develop their digital skills and learn how to interact in the virtual as well as in the physical space. Once we know that all students have what they need, we can provide learning opportunities for students to use digital tools whenever it is appropriate and will serve to enhance the instruction in our classroom.

Preparing for the Future

Many classrooms in the world today rely heavily on the use of technology, especially for higher education and schools that offer cyber courses to their students. In preparing students for the future, while we cannot predict their next steps when they leave our schools, we can do our best to prepare them with the right skills they need to navigate and thrive in this highly connected world.

How many times have students asked you when they will need the content that they are learning in your classroom? Think of your own experiences in school. Did you ever wonder when you might use something you learned in science or math or why you had to read a certain book in an English course? We might think we won't pursue a certain profession or use a specific skill, but the thing is, we don't ever really know what the future holds. Interests change, and opportunities come up. Opportunities are everywhere. It is difficult to predict what students might do when they leave our schools. The best we can do is to supplement the content by implementing different tools and strategies that will help students acquire additional skills that will become part of their future. We guide them just enough and provide them with support to chart their own learning path and develop skills that will help them to be successful with whatever they decide to do.

BUT HOW? We can do this by finding a way to build on the traditional work that our students are already doing in the classroom, but differently and innovatively. Chances are that students regularly create presentations and projects for their courses. Traditional presentation materials like paper and markers are effective for kinesthetic learners, as hands-on creating leads to authentic and meaningful learning and content retention. However, sometimes, we can go beyond simply engaging students in learning more by using technology. The technology might just be a catalyst to spark curiosity and push students to seek new ways to extend the possibilities for learning. In courses with curriculum focused on technology, whether a tech education course, computer science, or a business course, we should be offering multiple opportunities for students to create multimedia presentations and collaborate online.

THINK BACK TO THE "TECHNOLOGY" that was used when you went to school. Were movies shown using the big movie projector, with big movie reels that sometimes broke in the middle of the film? Or did you have to listen to cassette tapes or records in class? How about having to type reports on a typewriter without the availability of correcting tape? So many wasted pieces of paper! These were part of my learning experiences for most of my elementary and secondary education years. Imagine if we were still using these tools in our classrooms.

For many years in the traditional classroom, there were not many options for technology to supplement instruction. In the late 1990s, there was a rise in new digital tools for learning. Students could create by using word processing tools and presentation tools like Power-Point, but even then, whether due to a lack of resources or a lack of teacher preparation, they were still not commonplace in classrooms. My first PowerPoint presentation had twenty slides stored on ten disks, each requiring a few minutes to start up and leaving less time to present in class. Fortunately, our tech has advanced so much that we don't lose valuable instruction time with these tools. Maybe, for this reason, educators today might feel as though they are not qualified enough to implement technology tools in the classroom or simply that it's not part of what their position involves. Perhaps even some of the hesitancy is because there isn't training provided for all teachers as part of professional development, so that might hold some teachers back from trying new tools. It's time to diverge from that thinking.

We can't teach KIDS WIFI with landline strategies.

ADAM WELCOME, AUTHOR   @STEINBRINKLAURA

When it comes to professional development and stretching ourselves in ways that we either feel uncomfortable or may feel adversely about, things can be a bit difficult. Have you ever led a professional development session where you shared an idea or a tool that you were really excited about, only to be met by one or two, or possibly more colleagues, who bring up the negatives, push back, and sometimes push back a lot? It seems that in many schools, at least one teacher, if not more, are focused only on the tried-and-true traditional methods they have been using for years. They may be either apprehensive or simply have their minds made up that they don't need to make any changes to what they are doing. Things have worked just fine, so why do anything differently? I've heard it, my students have heard it, and without a doubt, it can be tough to change habits sometimes. But if we don't try, we risk missing out on opportunities that will positively impact our students. We must find a way to make a connection and engage in a conversation where each person feels that their opinion matters. We don't want to push for compliance. We want our colleagues to feel valued and have choices. The same that we want for our students.

❄

As there are different types of learners and learning preferences, there are different groups of people identifiable based on their interest or aversion to technology. Everett Rogers, an American sociologist, came up with the "Diffusion of Innovation Theory" and five groups of people, reflective of how they accept change. (1962, 2003). He defined them as: Innovators, Early Adopters, Early Majority, Late Majority, or the Laggards. As you read the descriptions which follow, think about your colleagues or members of your PLN and see if you can identify them based on these groups.

- Innovators and early adopters are interested in taking risks and finding new ways to change from their traditional teaching methods. Innovators are more likely to go out and acquire that new device or try something right away, whereas the early adopters may wait a little bit before diving in.
- The Early Majority and Late Majority are not entirely against making changes or trying the new tool, but tend to wait a bit longer before joining in, possibly waiting to see if the new tool or initiative will last. They are good at wait time and don't necessarily want to dive into something that will disappear before they have a chance to implement it.
- The Laggards are typically the more conservative and traditional teachers. Members of this group are fine with continuing the way they have been teaching (the way they've always done it) and do not see needs nor benefits for using these new tools.

Which group do you identify with? Keep that in mind and see if any of it resonates with you and the experiences you've had. Try to think about the teachers you work with, or even some of your students, and where they might fall in these groups. Understanding who they are helps us to know how to address the needs and concerns of all.

SEEM like the groups are far apart? Maybe, but the common ground among these seemingly distant beliefs lies in doing what is best for the students. When we take our own personal opinions out of the equation and can talk about the why behind wanting to try something that might seem like a risk, we make progress. If we work together to analyze the purpose as to how it might enhance and improve the learning experience and potential for students, we will find a way to work together. It's amazing what can happen simply by making time to openly talk and express our opinions in a collaborative nature, and by focusing on our *why*. Our why means doing what is best for our students. And sometimes that means pulling ourselves out of the equation and thinking specifically about what needs to happen for the benefit of student learning.

PROGRESS WILL BE MADE, because focusing on how we can positively impact and benefit our students is at the heart of everything we do. They are the reason we do what we do. Even if we don't particularly favor the use of technology or adding a new teaching strategy into our practice, we need to keep our minds open to the potential for learning. Being mindful that while it might be something that does not necessarily benefit us, it isn't about us. We are in the business of doing what is best for others. Of preparing ourselves to be our best. Always remember, "the future of the world is in our classrooms today," and we can't prepare by only sharing what we know and limit it to our own skills. We must create opportunities for students to surpass our knowledge and skills and encourage them to build their own so that they can come back and teach us as well.

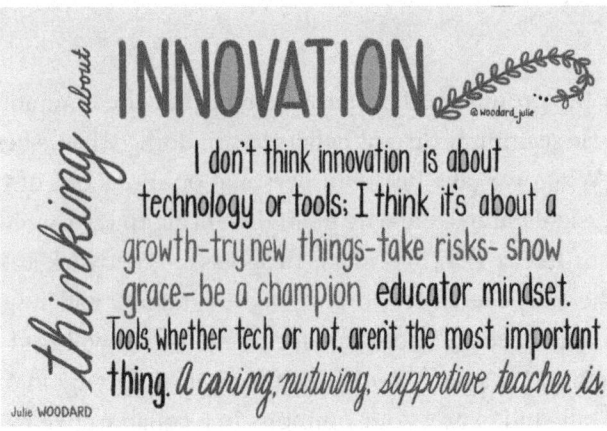

thinking about

INNOVATION
@ Woodard_julie

I don't think innovation is about technology or tools; I think it's about a growth-try new things-take risks- show grace-be a champion educator mindset. Tools, whether tech or not, aren't the most important thing. *A caring, nurturing, supportive teacher is.*

Julie WOODARD

Looking at Ourselves

Now it's time to decide where you fit in this continuum when it comes to innovation and breaking tradition. Do you welcome new ideas? How do you feel about the yearly initiatives that schools become involved in? Sometimes people may be apprehensive about trying new things because prior experience shows that the lifespan of similar tools and methods in the classroom or in the school has been short-lived. It's understandable why some teachers may not want to invest the time to learn something new, especially if it is more advanced or out of their comfort zone. Perhaps they feel that the tool or the strategy will not be consistently implemented or enhance instruction, so they don't buy in too easily to change. Or knowing that technology sometimes changes quickly, they decide to not take a chance of learning something for nothing. For this group of teachers, time might be better spent working on the more traditional methods and tools, especially when we have the belief and evidence that support the effectiveness of these. However, we owe it to students to challenge ourselves and model lifelong learning by stepping out of our own comfort zones.

❄

Now here comes the hard part. If you were to place yourself somewhere on the "Everett" continuum, assigning yourself one of these labels, which one would you be?

- Would you consider yourself to be an innovator?

Someone who is not only interested in finding the newest tools or coming up with innovative ways to use older technology tools in your classroom, but actively seeking new resources to try? Even working to share your ideas with colleagues and try them out in your classroom?

- Or are you somewhere in the middle?

You are moderately interested in the tech, but still holding back some, invested in building skills, hesitant to take that big jump?

- Or are you at the far end, a Laggard?

You have your own resources and methods, and they work well for you and your students. Why change?

While you may not be an innovator or an early adopter, perhaps you hover in the middle, holding on to the traditional ways you've always done things to be safe, but you are interested in exploring the other options available. You are still opening yourself up to change. However, if you are on the latter end of the continuum, you may be skeptical of the new tool or have your mind made up that the way you have chosen to do things in your classroom, whether or not that involves any technology at all, has worked and will continue to work and you don't need to change. For people who provide professional development and even school leaders, those who fall into this group may be met with mixed feelings. But this can change.

I would hope that in schools today, we would not find many "laggards" because if so, it means that the students are being limited to the knowledge and skill level of the teacher. When they are limited, they do not have an opportunity to explore and find their own passions and interests beyond what they are directly being taught when it comes to the curriculum. We need to work together, pull in these groups more closely, because there is always something to learn, and we all have room to grow.

We need to help students take steps out of their comfort zones, and that means we need to model this as part of who we are. Think about your own interests when it comes to technology and ask yourself if you are an early adopter or do you relate better with the laggards. We need to consider what makes teachers feel this way and how we can work together to change it. What steps could you take next month to help a laggard set aside their concerns and take one step forward for the sake of students? It starts with us, being the change and putting ourselves out there for what we believe in. Our students.

Knocking Down Barriers

In working toward a master's degree in educational technology, much of my research focused on online learning and motivation and explored the reasons that people resist change when it comes to technology. Learning about Peggy Ertmer, a professor at Purdue, taught me about the reasons people are sometimes hesitant to use technology. She referred to these as "first- and second-order barriers." First-order barriers means there is a problem with the device itself, or the type of technology is a bit difficult to use and requires additional instruction. Second-order barriers are focused on the person and their resistance to trying a technology or not believing there is value in technology use in their classroom. Working with a first-order barrier can be done through coaching, working with peers, and even having students work with teachers to show them technology tips. It can be a bigger challenge to resolve the second-order barriers because they focus closely on the personal beliefs of the teacher. Therefore, it may be difficult to try to bring about change in their perception of the technology and get them more involved. An effort needs to be made to pull them into a conversation and develop a relationship in which concerns can be shared, questions can be answered, and a common ground and starting point can be found (Ertmer, 1999). The first step is determining why the hesitancy exists, whether support is needed in terms of learning the technology or if common ground needs to be found. At times, teachers on opposite ends of the continuum have been paired and created something new that leaves them feeling positive and excited to make changes in the classroom.

"We are getting somewhere: It does not matter how slowly you go, as long as you do not stop (keep on moving)."

CONFUCIUS, CHINESE TEACHER

Change takes time, and, of course, it can be frustrating whether you are the one who wants to change or you are pushing back against it. Remember to keep perspective on the purpose of the change, not simply whether or not you want it. We are committed to doing what is best for students, and that means taking ourselves out of the equation. While it might require extra time or stepping out of our comfort zone, trying things that we are not sure will work, we all have to be risk-takers. Being the risk-takers, we will project a good model for our students and our peers. We will show that we are invested in doing what's best for all learners, and we narrow the distance between us, students, and teachers, when it comes to change.

Without a doubt, some concerns are understandable with so many digital tools available, and the common sentiment that there is a lack of time in a teacher's day. It might seem like it's just too much additional information and unnecessary resources to take on. How can there be enough time to learn how to use, to create, and to implement new materials on top of the work we are already doing in our classrooms?

Fortunately, with many of the digital tools today, many resources are available to teachers. There are possibilities for collaborating with colleagues in the development of different activities and learning materials for classes. The idea is not about layering something else on top of the curriculum; it is about weaving it together by adding in some tech. Take just one step in a different direction. The worst thing that can happen is you might have to rethink a strategy or look for a different tool, but it is a risk worth taking.

A Plan to Tech It Up

Coming up with a way to meet everyone's interests and specific needs can be a challenge. One of the best ways to go about it is by focusing on the relationships first. Relationships are critical, whether it's the relationships with our students or with our colleagues. If we start by trying to connect an innovator with a laggard, it might be difficult to find a comfortable meeting point. The innovator will be eager to use the technology, whereas the laggard may be hesitant and have doubts. But there are ways we can work together to draw upon these uncertainties to promote collaboration between the groups.

As a comparison, think about any type of peer tutoring or collaborative learning that you may use in your classroom. How do you typically group your students? Perhaps you allow them to choose their partners, you may create the groups randomly, or you make specific choices based on certain criteria such as student interest or student levels of mastery of the content. When trying to engage more teachers in learning about technology and helping them to feel more comfortable, we need to think about how to connect them with a supportive colleague. And when time is an issue, what are some other ways that we can create learning experiences that will enable us to go beyond what we already know and explore what else is out there?

Create a Network

1) **Digital learning Co-ops**: One idea that may work well, especially if finding a common meeting time is difficult, or teachers may not be ready to take on a lot of new ideas or technology tools, is to create a "Digital Learning Co-op." If you are a Tech coach or an administrator, and you have some "innovators" or "early adopters" among your faculty, think about how to connect them with other members of your team and work together.

First, seek their advice for a list of some digital tools that do not require a lot of preparation time, and that will apply to different content areas and levels. Personally, I usually try to recommend a few different types, such as a game-based learning tool, an interactive tool, and one more for creation. My recommendations in these areas are Gimkit, Nearpod, and Buncee, because of the benefit for students and our experience together.

The next step would be to determine who to pair members of your faculty with so that they can learn about the technology together. You may not get a 100% participation rate, and sometimes it can be hard to get teachers to volunteer with many things already on their plate. Maybe at the start, ask for a few volunteers to try out the digital co-op idea. When you have a few groups, set a period of time for them to work together and plan time to discuss their thoughts and takeaways.

How to set **up digital co-ops**: One suggestion is to pair up an "early adopter" and a "laggard," task them to come up with a teaching method or an instructional format that they both use and to think about how they could enhance it with technology. How can they connect? You could ask the innovators to come up with a list of tools that they recommend, and the "co-ops" can work together or work independently to try out the tool with their classes.

It is important to have a time where everyone can meet together, even if only briefly to share the benefits they found, areas where maybe a change is needed, and a time to make suggestions about where to go from there. Most importantly, keep the focus on the purpose and evaluating whether or not there were any improvements, and the perception of each member of the co-op. See if either "side" has changed their way of thinking as a result of having worked together, and if so, how? This might be an area to then start with for the next time. Maybe there was an activity that led to a change in the mind of the more reluctant teacher. Maybe the tool opened up more opportunities for learning for the students or freed up some of the clerical time that was required before. Whatever the benefits and even the negative points are, those who are participating in this adventure should openly share and reflect their experiences.

We can only "do better when we know better," as Maya Angelou said, and so we need to share our experiences and tell our stories so that we can help others who are in similar situations or have the same experiences that we do. Together we are better!

2) **Student Tech Teams:** Any time that I have taken students to educational technology conferences to present, educators have been highly complimentary of my students. They comment on how professional and knowledgeable the students are and how the students' excitement for learning is contagious. Students should have opportunities to share the work they are doing in the classroom and use their skills to help others learn. An idea that can be beneficial for teachers and students would be the creation of a student "Tech Team."

While schools have their own IT departments, they may not have tech coaches available to assist when teachers have technology questions or are looking for ideas on new instructional methods and tools. Having a group of students serve on a Tech Team is an ideal way to promote collaboration, to offer opportunities for more interactions, and to continue building important relationships for learning.

To set this up, find out which students might be interested and if there is time available, whether before or after the school day or during a study hall even. During this time, establish a designated place for the "tech team," where students are available to answer questions and to help a teacher. The assistance from the tech team should not be limited to teachers. Encourage peers to seek out the help of their classmates, especially in preparing students for the future, whether it be for learning or for work after graduation.

CREATING an opportunity like this is beneficial for students to develop soft skills. The soft skills they need for the future include communication, collaboration, problem-solving, and time management, to name a few. The setup will also help to develop their leadership skills. To get started:

- Create a survey to see if teachers are interested and preferred days and times.
- Find students who are interested in technology (recommend some students who you know would benefit from this confidence booster).
- Set up a space that is accessible throughout the day as well as before and after school.
- Provide the right devices and technology materials.
- Share the schedule with the staff and students. Post it near the Tech space.
- Follow up with teachers and students and have a feedback form to submit after working with the tech team.

Give it a try, and if it goes well, consider expanding the concept into a course in which students participate in project-based learning and develop entrepreneurial skills. Students, as well as teachers, will benefit, and students will gain valuable skills for the future.

3) **Tech Tip Tuesdays or Wi-Fi Wednesdays:**

Many of the opportunities available for professional development training involve bringing people in from different organizations to run the trainings. However, not every faculty member might be able to attend these sessions, or some might not find value in the specific tool or method being presented. Thinking back again to that "continuum" ranging from the innovators to the laggards, how would these different groups likely evaluate their experience in one of these sessions? Would one session in a "one-size-fits-all" type of delivery benefit all of the members of the faculty? Probably not.

Why not involve teachers by encouraging them to share how they use technology and offering some tips and tricks? See if you can find some who are interested in leading a "Tech Tip Tuesday" or "Wi-Fi Wednesday session."

OFFER a short session held either before or after school or during a common planning time, when teachers can stop by and learn a quick tip or try a new tool. Keeping these sessions short, perhaps 15 to 30 minutes, and using a variety of tools might just lead to more teacher engagement with integrating technology in the classroom. Teachers do not have a lot of extra time during the school day and may not be too excited to stay after school for a long session of professional development, but a shorter session with one or two quick ways to get started might just be the answer.

CREATE a survey to determine interest in these sessions. Use either a Google or Microsoft form to create a survey and ask teachers to submit ideas or to respond to some prompts about the types of tools or areas of focus they want to learn more about, and their availability. Once you have this information, you can either send a separate survey to find teachers who might be interested in leading the sessions or save time by including that as one of the questions in the original survey. To help with the information, perhaps involve your department chairs or faculty leaders, depending on your school if you have these types of faculty advisor groups. When doing something like this for the first time, there's always room to grow, and definitely, changes can be made. The idea is to just get started with something that will lead to benefits for all learners. It may be a risk because it's something new, but we know the benefits of taking these risks. We can anticipate some pushback or an initial lack of interest, or conversely, a ton of interest, which leads you to think about expanding the concept to offer something another day of the week!

BUT FIRST, decide how to set up these learning sessions. Some ideas might involve reaching out to local schools or even members of your PLN, to see if they have these types of activities happening in their schools. Because technology is amazing and creates many diverse learning possibilities, even teachers who may have to leave at the end of the day or have other commitments could participate in a few different ways.

1. If the teacher leading the session does not mind being recorded, a short video can be created and shared so it can be watched whenever convenient. Using this approach is practical because it offers the availability of a tech lesson beyond just that one day or one session of PD. Creating sessions and recording them can be a good way to provide feedback to peers regarding teaching and delivering professional development sessions. An opportunity like this might just be a stepping stone to give a teacher the confidence needed to go out and present at a conference or in a nearby school. The more we share our knowledge, the more we learn too.

2. If a teacher is interested in leading a session but is not

available to stay after school, a good alternative is to create a short, interactive lesson or video and enable other educators to learn through the virtual learning space. Through technology, we are no longer limited or bound by time and space. For teachers working in different schools within the same district, this setup works well because they can still participate without having to leave their own school to attend. It can be tough to break away from school at the end of the day, sometimes with meetings, students staying after for help, or just preparing our classrooms. A recorded, on-demand session might lead to more participation because there is no longer a requirement to travel between schools or to extend the school day beyond its regular time.

3. If we want to not only build our network in terms of using technology, we could build our PLN by connecting teachers from our school with other educators in nearby or global communities. Imagine the power of learning when we connect globally to learn together and bring in new experiences and connections for our students. Get started with EduMatch, joining ISTE or a state affiliate, or connect with programs through Microsoft EDU or Google.

We are all learners, and everyone has something to teach, and we all have something to learn. Designing these types of activities not only builds on the professional and technical skills of students and teachers, but adds more opportunities to continue building the relationships that are the foundation for learning and for personal and professional growth.

A Tech Adventure

Something to keep in mind is that you might receive a little pushback. Some teachers simply feel comfortable using the same methods or don't have enough information about how to select the right technology. Not everyone is familiar with the technology integration frameworks, so maybe taking the time to explain one of the well-known frameworks such as SAMR (Substitution, Augmentation, Modification, Redefinition), or TPACK (Technology, Pedagogical and Content Knowledge) and explaining how they work would be beneficial. A Tech Coach could explain and show some examples quickly. Using this as a guide will help teachers understand how to make one small change in what they're already doing that will lead to a bigger impact on student learning.

We need to be mindful of the comfort level of our teachers and work together to draw upon the technology skills of our colleagues and our students. We are co-learners, and by collaborating in one of these ways, we convey that every member of the school is valued and can be a leader. Before deciding on any one tool or any one of these ideas, make sure that the technology is used purposefully.

Reflect

Think about some of your favorite activities or lessons that you have done with your students. What makes them *your* favorite? How did your students feel about them? Think about some that did not go well, and maybe some topics that you struggled to make engaging for students. Taking on too many new ideas can be overwhelming, but if you think about the best, the worst, and the middle ground, you might just come up with one solid direction to go in.

ASK YOURSELF: What is something that takes up a lot of my time? More specifically, what takes time away from being able to either provide timely and meaningful feedback to the students, or promote student communication and interactions with one another? We need to keep the lines of communication open between students and us, and between students and their peers. We can create a lot of opportunities by using technology to enhance and extend the learning possibilities. Communication is facilitated better through newsletters, blogs, websites, messaging apps, and social media.

WE HAVE to leverage technology in a way that fosters the creation of opportunities for students, to extend our own learning, and to continuously improve together. It is helping students to understand more than just information—it's about what to do with that information, how to process the content, and how to expand their thinking to apply it in different ways. Choose one way to empower students to lead and be okay with them taking more control and driving their learning.

#THRIVEinEDU

Once you decide on one of these activities, share how you set up your Tech Team or share a picture of Tech Tuesday or Wi-Fi Wednesday events and use the hashtag #THRIVEinEDU.

8 EXPLORING THE WORLD BEYOND OUR CLASSROOM

A New World of Learning

Do you remember when Bill and Ted went on their "Excellent Adventure?" The movie *Bill and Ted's Excellent Adventure* is about two high school students trying to avoid enrollment in a military school and failing their history course, by traveling through the past in a telephone time machine. Bill and Ted travel through time to collect all of the historical figures they can to prepare the "ultimate" history presentation.

Wow, imagine what it would be like to interact and learn directly from some famous people in history, rather than reading about them in a book or seeing videos! Imagine going back in time to places like ancient Greece, France during the middle ages, or experience life during the 13th century in China. What an impact to learn from people like Socrates, brave the battlegrounds with Napoleon, fight alongside Genghis Khan, or watch 18-year-old Joan of Arc leading the French army to victory over the English! Experience life in the wild west by hanging out with Billy the Kid, appreciate classical music by hearing Beethoven play the piano, and understand the country's history by listening to Abraham Lincoln deliver the Gettysburg Address. What if all students could create something to share their learning like this? Wouldn't it lead to a more meaningful way to learn and retain the information! Could you imagine having the opportunity to learn like this, traveling back in time, or traveling to another place and exploring on your own? Consider the impact this kind of exploration would have on students to make their learning more engaging and authentic!

The Need to Explore!

Think about a topic or a unit that you teach every year, that even for you—the one who is so passionate about teaching—even *you* have become a bit bored with it. It happens.

Maybe you've been brainstorming ideas of how to "cover" it, asking colleagues and students for new ideas, maybe you have tried different strategies, and it still comes across the same way it always has: boring. Think about the number of times that teachers assign worksheets, reading passages, or projects, that have students basically replicating the exact same product or simply asking questions that have only one correct, intended answer. We provide information and ask our students to give it right back to us. Now think about some topics that you cover in your course, ones in which you have asked students to just "imagine" they were there. What would it be like to travel to a certain place, live during a certain time, or even to process or visualize how something might work by immersing in a new learning environment? Explore the wonders of the world, outer space, different cultures, and more. Imagine how much you could enhance some of the topics that you cover, especially those that even you are not too excited about anymore.

EVERYBODY LOVES YOUTUBE, right? Maybe you have scoured YouTube for videos, created your own lessons using some of the many technology tools available, adding in personal stories and other authentic materials that you think of, to make it more than just a video. If all of these ideas sound like good ways to provide a variety of learning opportunities for students, they are. Don't get me wrong, there are a lot of tools to promote learning and student engagement. They should supplement the course, not be the only tool or resource used. And while it can be difficult to figure out where to start, the problem here lies not in the "what"; it lies in the "who."

Who is creating the learning product? It is often said that the person doing the talking is the one doing the learning. It likely holds true that the person who is doing most of the creating is also the one doing most of the learning. It is the reinforcement and repetitiveness of interacting with the content that leads to mastery. We get used to being in the lead and making the decisions in the classroom. As teachers, we do this often, which is how we continue to develop our skills and retain knowledge about many topics over the years. The same would apply to our students. The more that we have students interacting with the content and learning on their own terms, the more we increase the amount of learning that happens. If you are a teacher who talks and creates the class materials most of the time, you are most likely an expert at the content, but we need to help our students acquire that knowledge. We need to help our students become the experts and support them as they create new problems to solve and ways to learn.

Recharge with new ideas

It's okay if we need to take time to recharge our own motivation for learning. When we teach the same content, we can fall into a habit of using similar methods and class materials. Yet consider other innovative and creative ideas. Of course, traditional and "conventional" ways exist, but I guess that you've tried those, and you are looking for something to better grab the attention of your students as well as yourself. Let's do something unconventional. Let's create unreal experiences that will immerse students in learning, boost motivation and engagement, and lead to better learning outcomes for students. Who knows? After adding in some of these different ideas, you might not find it so cumbersome to cover that topic any longer, whether because students created something that can be used and repurposed for future classes, or because (and this is highly likely) the students uncovered new knowledge and ended up teaching you in the process. Either way, the results will lead to better learning for everyone and might even be the catalyst needed to recharge our motivation for learning and growing.

A Plan to Immerse Students in Learning

Looking to solve the puzzle of student engagement? Many educators might look to technology as the answer. Without a doubt, many possibilities are available, but we have to remember to stay focused on our purpose, asking ourselves why we want to use a certain tool and what we believe the benefits will be. Sometimes technology is the answer, especially when it can connect students with more immersive learning experiences. Technology can be the catalyst to hook students into a lesson just enough until their curiosity sets in, motivation takes over, and their level of engagement climbs. If students feel as though they're interacting with the content or if it opens up the possibility to learn beyond the classroom, to explore global connections and learn from others around the world, this is purposeful use of technology. Just think about the possibilities. We can connect students with people and places that students might never encounter, had it not been for the development of the many tools for learning and exploring the world. If you don't teach a technology class and this feels somewhat unconventional, even better. Let's get started and explore! Let's make the world our classroom!

1) Field Trips: Everybody loves field trips. Sometimes students are just excited to get out of the classroom and school building to go somewhere and see what's going on in the world. Unfortunately, field trips cannot be taken as frequently as educators may prefer. One of the common problems facing schools today is the lack of funding. Many resources that students and educators need in their classrooms cannot be obtained because of inadequate resources. But with a little bit of creative thinking, there are ways we can find solutions for very little if any cost at all. Wouldn't it be nice if we could take our students around the world on a trip, give them opportunities to explore different environments, learn about different spaces, focus on scientific or historical explorations at any time? We can! Imagine the impact on student and teacher learning, as we all explore together in our classroom.

Without a doubt, there probably would be a lot of field trips planned by educators in every school. Because funding is an issue, and taking students out of classes too often can negatively impact overall learning, we need suitable alternatives. Although these alternatives might not be as exciting as exploring in person, they still will be beneficial for students. If funding and making travel plans are tough, how about setting up some Virtual Field Trips for students? Implementing digital tools to create a scavenger hunt using images, 360 videos, and other content, including even ones students create, can be of tremendous benefit for learning. When students set the pace for learning and control how they explore, it truly does make a difference. It's about finding the right tool to set this up, and it's something that can be done easily with a long-lasting impact on student learning. Get started with Google Expeditions and Google Tour Creator!

2) Augmented and Virtual Reality

Have you learned more about outer space by exploring it? What would it be like to work from the Oval Office? Ever think about spending the day in Africa, watching the elephants or zebras closely, so close that you feel they are running around you? These would be amazing experiences for students rather than simply watching videos or looking at photos. Think back to the different courses where you had to interact with something like a 3D object, examine parts of the body, or try to get a decent understanding of something by looking at a one-dimensional photo or watching a video. Often in science or health classes, students learn about molecules or anatomy, in math about shapes, and in social studies about famous people and places in history. How many times were you, as a student, given a project and assigned to create something to demonstrate your understanding? Who didn't love creating those volcano replicas or other projects that required things like marshmallows and toothpicks, popsicle sticks, paint, or maybe the traditional construction paper, poster boards, markers, even glitter, just to name a few typical materials? There is absolutely nothing wrong with these conventional ways to have students create in the classroom. Hands-on, active learning fueled with student choice is powerful, and students learn best this way.

The authenticity that emerges in each of these student-designed products is invariably impressive. We can learn a lot about students and their creativity by allowing them to explain their "take" on the learning concept. But how about giving them an opportunity to interact with the content differently? Students can see the layers of an object by moving through them, or stepping into another world by using a portal to explore a faraway place. Imagine being able to escape into another land, instantly, all from the classroom seat. The power of taking those virtual trips and diving into the learning more is tremendous. Beyond having students consume the content, we can have students create 3D objects, virtual tours, and adventures. We can also promote the development of communication skills and creativity by having students narrate a story about what they saw during their field trips and explorations.

Let's dive into new worlds of learning

The use of augmented and virtual reality is becoming increasingly more popular in the world, especially in K-12 classrooms and higher education. It can be difficult to keep up with so much, especially when there are new stories shared every day about how these tools are being used to train professionals in different industries, and how students are not only learning through these tools but also creating and going far beyond where the traditional classroom lesson plans can take them. For some educators, the thought of bringing these tools in might seem too time-consuming; however, many resources are available to get started. One place to start is with Jaime Donally, founder of ARVRinEDU and author of the book *"Learning Transported."* Jaime is constantly adding more to her site and during her weekly Twitter chat on Wednesday nights. She is the first person I reach out to when I have questions about anything related to AR/VR.

There's always a concern about the benefits of different technology tools, and these tools should not be used simply because they are the latest trend. Understandably, educators and parents will be curious to know the specific benefits and purposes of choosing these tools over more conventional ones for student learning. We must leverage technology purposefully and take time to explore the different ways to implement them effectively into the classroom, involving students and parents in the conversation. When it comes to choosing digital tools, we should consider whether they provide something more authentic for learning, allow opportunities for the creation of or availability of innovative learning spaces for students, and lead to a transformation in learning experiences.

❄

THESE TECHNOLOGIES PROVIDE powerful opportunities for students to closely explore, interact, manipulate objects and content, and "travel" to previously unreachable places. By using some of these AR/VR tools, we give students more control in how and where they are learning and in ways that the traditional tools of textbooks, pictures, and videos cannot. Imagine the level of student engagement if they are told they could immediately "travel" to anywhere in the world. What would they think about the chance to explore outer space, looking down on the earth, having the solar system surround them, or taking off in the space shuttle? Giving students the chance to come up with their own questions while exploring, to become more curious for learning, will promote student agency and be more meaningful for students. By using these tools, we promote digital equity so that all students have an opportunity to explore and interact in their own way.

How do I start?

As the teacher, it can be a challenge to keep up with so many new tools and know which are compatible with student devices or school networks. Some steps to get started:

- Make time to talk with students about their interests, giving them the chance to create and giving you the chance to learn from them. It's okay to not know everything!
- Take a risk in learning these tools and push through some of the challenges, so you can better understand how to help students as they create their own AR/VR projects.
- Choose one or two tools to start with, find ready-made content, and try with your students or teachers. Give it some time, evaluate the benefits, and keep moving forward. "See" how it goes!

WE NEED to be prepared for student questions and offer some (but not too much) help, because students need to learn, to problem-solve, and to develop these skills on their own. When we implement some new, unconventional tools and technologies in our classroom, we show students that we are interested in taking some risks with ways to learn, which is a good model to demonstrate.

HERE ARE a few versatile tools and ideas for using them. They each offer options for classroom use as well as ready-made examples that can help you to get started right away.

Quickstarts!

Nearpod is a good way to start exploring the world from your classroom. Beyond its use as an interactive lesson for engaging students in different ways, there are virtual tours from around the world and 3D objects for students to explore more closely. Thousands of lessons are available to choose from, and creating a new lesson is easy for teachers and students. Take students on an interactive trip around the world using a tool like Nearpod. Students can be more than just consumers; they can create their own lessons to lead in the classroom. Taking a field trip to far-away countries and exploring previously unreachable landmarks are better ways to promote immersive learning.

DIGITAL STORYTELLING in 3D or augmented/virtual reality takes learning to a whole new level. Push boundaries by having students delve into their imagination and design an interactive story with animated characters or use a storyboard to create a choose-your-own-adventure activity to engage students with the content. Look into tools like **Metaverse** or **3DBear,** and give students the lead to create characters and place them into the learning environment or travel anywhere in the world. These are more creative, immersive, and student-driven ways to tell a story in augmented reality and get students excited for learning! Make time to check out **CoSpaces Edu** where students create different "spaces" in virtual reality. Creating with tools like 3DBear or CoSpaces promotes collaboration as students can work together in a group to illustrate and narrate a story, create a game, and build anything they want. It can be a wonderful way to provide students with more authentic ways to demonstrate learning while building technology skills for the future and have fun in the process. How awesome would it be to walk through a space they created and use it to spark curiosity for learning and student engagement?

MERGEVR IS a holographic cube that enables the user to hold and interact with different 3D objects in their hands. The Merge cube can be used with apps for exploring outer space, the human body, biology-related topics and more. It can also be used in conjunction with CoSpaces, where students design their space and then can hold it in their hands.

3) Global Peer Collaborations

Think back to when you were a student. How did you learn about other cultures and different customs of people around the world? Maybe you learned by looking at pictures in the book or watching a video. Maybe you even had to create a project or do your own research. How often did you have the opportunity to actually connect with someone from the place or culture you were studying? Could you ask specific questions of someone who lived during a certain period or event? Chances are your learning was limited to the resources available within the classroom from your teachers, or the local library or community resources.

Did you ever sign up to have a pen pal from a different country? Years ago, corresponding with a pen pal took quite some time. It is so different now. Today there are many digital tools for connecting fairly quickly, enabling students to communicate with students from around the world at any time. Some people do not realize that this is even possible. There are many options out there, but it has not always been that way. In the past, sending a letter and waiting for a response could take weeks, if not months, depending on geographical locations. I remember one of my students in Spanish V sent a letter to a penpal in Argentina and never got a response, but received her unopened letter back more than one year later. Where was it? We have a much different experience today. We can find educators from around the world and make these penpal connections a possibility for our students in no time at all. Even better, we can use some of these AR/VR tools to explore our countries and collaborate on designing a new space using CoSpaces.

Do you remember the first time you met someone, and you could tell they were not from the same area as you? Maybe it was because of an accent when they spoke, the words they used, the way that they dressed, or how they interacted with you. Or maybe it was something else entirely. What were your initial thoughts? Did it make you curious to find out more about them and how their life compared to your own? Did you ask any questions about where they came from? We lose that opportunity when we walk away, and the conversation ends. Now more than ever, we have the opportunity to connect students globally so that they are not limited solely to learning that comes from reading a book or watching a video, or a chance meeting with someone from a different country. As educators, there is tremendous potential for us when we push the boundaries of our classroom space and show that learning from the world is possible. In today's world, we can no longer confine learning to the classroom or even the physical school space and class time. Let's work with students to explore and to build, connect, and develop their digital citizenship skills and make real-world connections.

How to do this

There are different learning communities out there that either formed because of a shared digital tool or became a PLN. These communities typically offer discussion boards where educators can connect with other classrooms around the world. It is easy to search and find a classroom for specific grade levels and content areas, or even based on a specific theme or topic of study. While specific digital tools may change with time, there will likely be an option available for setting up a fast and accessible way for students and educators to connect whenever it is convenient for them from wherever they are. Bringing the world of learning into your classroom and learning with the world will not only empower students to collaborate, to make authentic, meaningful peer collaborations, but will help them to develop soft skills as well. With access to different cultures and different perspectives, we promote curiosity for learning and develop empathy, and students become intrinsically motivated to seek more and do more by having control of their learning path.

For younger students, organizations like **Empatico** help educators from around the world set up class collaborations and offer resources to inform students about real-world issues. Leading students and educators to become globally connected and building a bridge between different cultures and background experiences should be part of each student experience. Many wonderful choices for facilitating close connections between students around the world exist. Using creative programs like **Buncee Buddies**, **Flipgrid** Pals, or doing a mystery **Skype** promotes global awareness and gives students a glimpse into learning around the world. Through these options, we connect students with real-world experts and pen-pals to learn and grow with.

Imagination and Exploration

Take some time to think about the methods and the tools you are currently using to amplify or facilitate student learning. What have you noticed about your choices and the impact on engaging students in learning? Which method or tool is making a difference in how, what, and where students learn? And remember, it does not have to be about the technology. It is about what you use to bring students in contact with the content and one another. Start with the suggestions in this chapter and think about which of these tools could be a substitute for something you are currently using, especially something that has only one purpose or typical use.

Decide whether to start with a virtual field trip or an augmented reality exploration. How can you hook students in and spark some curiosity? Make time to ask students for feedback and consider how you can engage students more in learning and create new opportunities for them to move from consumers to creators.

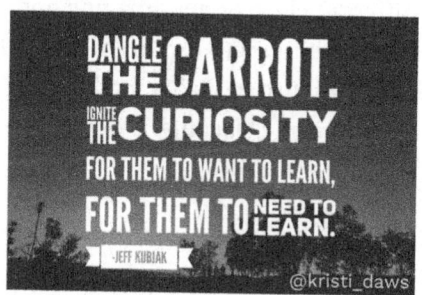

Quote by Jeff Kubiak from *In Other Words*, image by Kristi Daws.

Reflect

There are many ways we can immerse students in learning. Hands-on, student-driven activities amplify learning potential for students. Choosing tools for augmenting reality or escaping to far away previously unreachable places can empower students with new knowledge and authentic engagement. How could these changes impact your students and the way they learn? Think about all of your content knowledge and the potential for exchanging ideas and information with classrooms around the world. Involve students by asking students to choose a topic related to the content area and decide how they would like to learn more about it. Provide some options:

1. Do they want to create or participate in a scavenger hunt, go on a virtual field trip, or maybe find a global pen pal to exchange ideas, ask questions and share photos or videos?
2. Are your students creating a story or designing a space? Select one of the AR/VR tools for creating these interactive spaces and worlds. Task students to create scenes where they are telling a story, summarizing a movie or a book that they had read, or designing a different type of living space, environment, or any option of their choosing.
3. What is it like to travel to_____? Why not create a virtual tour of your town or set up an interview with students between two different classrooms? Imagine how much fun it would be for each classroom to explore what it's like to live in another place through virtual reality, and to have that personal connection while learning.

#THRIVEinEDU

Share a tour that students created or one that you went on as a class, or even post a screenshot of something created using augmented reality. Reflect on some of your takeaways and share some tips with other educators by using the hashtag #THRIVEinEDU.

NEVER doubt that a small group of thoughtful, committed citizens can change the WORLD; indeed it is the ONLY thing that EVER has.
~ Margaret Mead

A new PLP (Personal/Professional Learning Plan) with PLN and Mentoring

We have so much to learn from one another, and it doesn't matter whether we have years of experience behind us, or we are completely new to the profession or the school. We have heard or seen the phrases, "We are better together." There is often a perception that the more experience you have, the more you know and the less professional development you might need, and the other side, the less experience you have, the less you know and the more you need professional development. However, there is always room to grow professionally. The difficulty lies in finding the time, the resources, and making connections with educators to become part of a PLN with a PLP for PPD. Did you follow that?

Why do we have to keep learning?

Our profession requires that we keep learning, not just for ourselves but because of our responsibility to our students. The future — something we must be mindful of each day, especially at times where we might feel frustrated or like we are not making a difference. A quote that I keep in mind is:

"The future of the world is in my classroom today, a future with the potential for good or bad... Several future presidents are learning from me today; so are the great writers of the next decades, and so are all the so-called ordinary people who will make the decisions in a democracy...Only a teacher? Thank God I have a calling to the greatest profession of all! I must be vigilant every day, lest I lose one fragile opportunity to improve tomorrow."

IVAN WELTON FITZWATER

While we cannot truly know what lies in the future for our students (or ourselves) when it comes to the work that we do, there is one thing that we can be sure of: the need for ongoing professional learning. By exposing ourselves to different topics and pushing to understand more about the world, we can bring as much of the world to our students as we can. Our mission is to engage in and model ongoing professional learning so we can be the best version of ourselves for those we lead and learn with. Our challenge is to find the choices that meet our needs so we can meet theirs.

Finding What Works

When you hear the words "Professional Development," do you try to think of a way to get out of the PD that has been planned for you? Maybe not because you don't want to learn or have time to collaborate with colleagues, but rather it's the lack of personalized options available. Have you been hoping to design your own PD path, but know that the possibility of doing so is low? We don't ever know until we ask, right? So why not ask for the opportunity to design your own PLP (Personalized Learning Plan)? Think of the potential for personalized professional learning by visiting another school, offering to lead a PD session, and share your ideas, perhaps inviting students to present, running a book study, or anything that involves more individual choices. Educators need to advocate for their own learning needs and interests. We want this for our students, so let's get this for ourselves too.

What happens when you have questions or concerns and cannot find the time to reach out to other educators in your school or beyond? It is helpful to have a mentor. The traditional mentorship involves assigning new teachers to a mentor, typically an experienced member of the teaching staff. But something important to be mindful of is that we are always learning and have room to grow. Every educator needs a mentor, regardless of years of experience teaching or in the school. We are better when we draw upon our collective strengths and weaknesses to design the best learning experience for ourselves and then transfer this to our students.

IT'S NOT ALWAYS EASY. I remember reading a phrase in *Teach Like a Pirate* by Dave Burgess (2012) that resonated with me and hearing Dave speak about it at a presentation in Pittsburgh. He refers to the words "It comes easy to you ..." that other teachers would say to him when he taught. Many times, we may be perceived as having some expertise or knack for making something look simple to do. Some things come easy to me, at least that's how it seems to someone else. But most of the time, nobody really knows how much effort it takes. Our colleagues and our students do not know the amount of effort it took for us to come up with that new game, activity, teaching method, or anything we are doing in our classrooms. Even Michelangelo said, "If people knew how hard I had to work to gain my mastery, it would not seem so wonderful at all." So true. There are things that I try and repeatedly fail on my own, before deciding to give it a go in class. But I don't often share how much time I invested in getting things to work. There are exceptions though, like when students begin creating and start to struggle a bit, I will share how long it took for me to work it out on my own. Typically, I spend double or triple the amount of time that it takes them. Sometimes it makes all the difference just knowing that you aren't the only one to struggle with something.

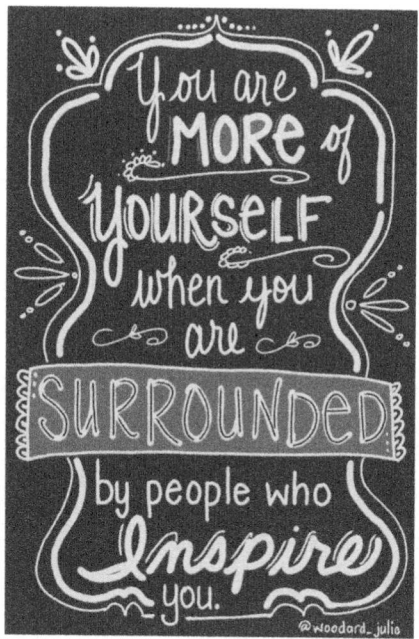

You don't have to be alone

Teaching can become an isolating profession. Depending on the type of school and daily teaching schedule, your day might pass by so quickly that you lack time to have meaningful interactions with your colleagues. Conversations can be hard to come by. With so many demands in the day, you may choose to eat lunch in your room to catch up on grading, prepare lessons for the next day, make phone calls to parents, or read in order to keep up with professional learning. Sometimes we choose to stay in isolation to enjoy moments of quiet and time to reflect and recharge, as the days are full of interactions, demands for our attention, and hundreds of mental tasks that can wear us out (but in a good way). It is important to find a way to balance between time spent in isolation where we take care of ourselves, and making time to connect with our colleagues and other educators, so we can take care of our professional selves as well.

Think of how you spend your typical day in school. Do you notice that you hardly even see the person that teaches next door to you or across the hall? Even with our best efforts to be present in the hallway and at the door greeting our students as they enter our classrooms, there's always so much going on with each class and each day that sometimes it is challenging to break away. We can create more opportunities to engage in professional conversations with peers and take a little time to unwind for a few minutes while standing at our classroom doors. We need to make sure that we are visible for our students, but in doing this, it often makes us invisible to our colleagues. In order to grow, we all need collaborations and support so we can continue building our skills as educators to be the best that we can be for our students and those we lead.

"The best teacher learning comes from seeing each other in practice."

LAINIE ROWELL

 The best teacher learning comes from seeing each other in practice.

 -Lainie Rowell

Observe Me

How many times have you been observed or had the opportunity to observe a colleague, either in your school or during a visit to another school? Chances are that you may not have many of these opportunities, but how wonderful it would be if we all had time to go out and explore one another's classrooms? How much could we learn by spending a few minutes in another classroom for part of a lesson? We can learn about our colleagues and their teaching style, learn more about students we may have in class and better understand their needs, and help one another by providing feedback. Doing even short observations is similar to the idea of the "#ObserveMe" movement, created by Robert Kaplinsky in 2016. Kaplinsky shared the reasoning behind the #ObserveMe movement, which is to work with peers to learn and grow together. We always have room to improve, and it benefits us to make these connections, to see others facilitating instruction in their classrooms, the activities that they are doing, the way the room is set up, and what goes into preparing and delivering a lesson for a day. The ObserveMe movement lets others know that we welcome guests into our classroom, want to have feedback and evaluations so that we can build on our own skills.

"Observe Me" is a movement happening in classrooms around the world that many educators are participating in. The Observe Me movement invites colleagues to visit other classrooms to observe teaching methods and provide specific feedback. How is this beneficial? It is a win-win for both the observer and the teacher being observed, as both will grow from the experience. Teacher observations can be scary, especially when done by administrators, and the thought of being "assessed" by our principals can cause some anxiety. But asking colleagues to enter our classrooms, and to focus on specific areas that we choose can only help us to grow. Besides having feedback about our teaching methods, it is a way to continue building our professional learning networks in a more meaningful way. Bethany Hill (@bethhill2829) is a principal in Arkansas who has shared her use of #ObserveMe in her school.

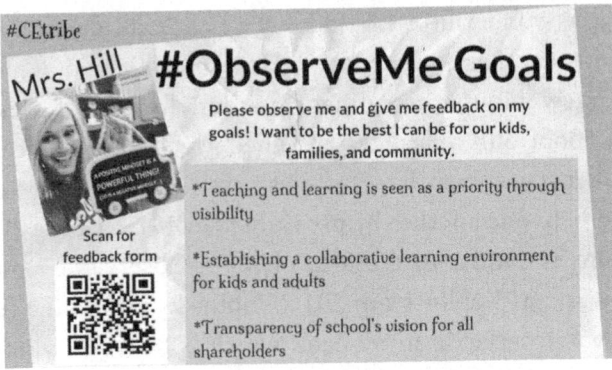

Image from Twitter, #CEtribe

We connect when we show our vulnerabilities and ask colleagues for help in building our professional skills. It is important to put ourselves out there, be open to feedback, and receptive to the ideas offered by peers. When we ask for specific, tangible feedback from our colleagues and set **SMART** (Specific, Measurable, Achievable, Realistic, Time-bound) goals, we can pursue areas of growth that are personal and relevant to our work. This practice benefits us as learners and as teachers. We can set goals, reflect, gather ideas after our yearly observations, and ask our students to provide us with feedback as well. But how often do we get to have these conversations? And why is it important that we make professional learning more accessible and an intentional part of our practice?

As educators, we must be in the constant pursuit of new knowledge, of building our skills in not only the content we teach, but also in acquiring whatever new skills will enable us to stay relevant in our practice and passionate in our profession. Professional development days are part of every teacher's calendar year. How often do teachers have the opportunity to suggest topics for professional development or to lead any of these sessions? Wouldn't it be ideal to design our own professional learning plan that provides more voice and choice in learning, just as we want for our students?

Opportunities are Everywhere

Take time to think about some of the activities that you do in your classroom. How often do you use technology? What is your comfort level when it comes to using technology or finding a new tool to try? How familiar are you with new trends, best practices, and innovative ideas, and how much professional support do you have in these each day? We all have a responsibility to develop our own skills so that we can provide more for our students. When we ask students to take risks in learning in our classrooms, we owe it to them to provide different options for them to show their learning beyond the basics and the traditional ways we have always used. Having students decide what kind of projects to create, as well as how to communicate and collaborate within the classroom and beyond the walls of our school, will better prepare them for the future.

We are no longer confined to learning in a specific space or time, nor from any particular person or role in education. We can connect instantly with educators from around the world or learn from students and colleagues in our school community. There are many quick ways to get started with building your own learning network. It simply takes deciding on one direction to head in and taking that first step. We must push beyond the walls of our schools and try some unconventional ways to learn, grow, and empower ourselves.

A Network for Others

The world is so big, yet so small. Years ago, our learning and our professional networks were limited to our school and nearby school communities. We only had time to connect within our schools or to interact at conferences periodically throughout the year. It took time to make those connections happen, and we were limited by the hours in our school day. Today, we have so many ways that we can connect beyond the physical space of our classrooms and schools, in our communities, throughout our states and even beyond our own countries, putting us in contact with educators globally within minutes. It is remarkable to think of what we are capable of today with technology. It enables us to escape isolation and bring in a world full of opportunities for our classrooms. Technology is extremely powerful for opening up new and innovative ways for educators to get and give support, and to be able to chart our own professional development path. Also, we can not only amplify our own learning, but we can also directly impact the students' learning.

But it is not completely about the technology, although this can be a catalyst for creating a network of learning in little to no time at all. Fostering asynchronous and synchronous interactions leads to more authentic connections for professional growth and in ways that match the time and physical constraints that often impede these professional collaborations. To receive the most benefits of what technology has to offer, we need some starting points. The most important is knowing how to find the right tools, which will prove to be versatile and provide educators with options for powerful forms of professional development and personal growth.

1) Voxer PLN: We often wish there was more time for longer conversations during the school day, later in the evening, or on the weekends. Finding time during the school day is tough because schedules are jam-packed. Sometimes even making a quick phone call or text messaging takes too much time. It is vital to our professional growth to be able to connect with our colleagues and others beyond our school community. Using something like Voxer or any other communication tool that enables asynchronous or synchronous communication can be extraordinarily helpful to educators.

In our practice, we need to reflect, and we need feedback as part of our professional development. There will be questions about best practices, how to handle classroom management issues, how to balance schedules, and focus on personal well-being. Sometimes educators just need to share frustrations in a safe space and know that they are not alone. Everyone needs a support system, but we often lack time to meet face to face, and even talking sometimes is a challenge, which is why the use of technology makes sense. It creates more opportunities for educators to escape any isolation they might be feeling, especially if it was a choice to become isolated in order to keep up with all of the professional duties. But how can we learn if we are alone?

When we leverage the right tools, like using Voxer or other messaging apps that provide live interactions, we have anytime access to global support and connectedness. It just takes that first step to get started. Find a tool and make a plan that works for you. Check out the many groups on Voxer.

Here are some ideas for using Voxer:

- Create a group chat with colleagues and use it for facilitating anytime, anywhere connections. Make time to talk with your colleagues and share experiences.
- Create a group chat on a specific topic for sharing ideas and asking questions. Some groups focus on blended learning, social-emotional learning, and augmented and virtual reality, to name a few.
- Create a book study. Set up a schedule, invite colleagues and PLN to join in, and be able to participate whenever you can. If you have tried Twitter and are looking for something different, explore the Voxer groups available for book studies and themed chats.

The power of connecting, access to support, ideas, and a PLN is right in our hands. We just need to find the right tool that works best for us and start building! Start with EduMatch!

2) Student-Teacher PLN Power: Have you ever been working with one of your students, maybe while they're completing an assignment or doing something on their phone, and you learn something new just during the interaction with them? Personally, I learned how to mass

delete images from the iPads rather than deleting every single image one by one. (Yes, I was deleting them individually for years). It was a transformative learning moment for me! There is much to learn from our students. Sometimes it is just something we notice from our interactions with others by taking the time to have conversations to find out how they learn best or which activities they enjoy, and think are the most beneficial in class. Asking for student input for project ideas or other classroom activities can be quite helpful and lead to students feeling valued. A student-teacher PLN may not be something commonly thought of; however, creating this unconventional type of a PLN will be mutually beneficial. Teachers will better understand and stay relevant to student needs and interests, and students will have support and learn the value of a PLN as they move through school and prepare for their future.

Ideas for a student-teacher PLN

A student-teacher PLN can be formally set up with time set aside before or after school or added in flexibly during the class as part of the learning experience. A time when students and teachers collaborate, ask each other questions, share ideas, talk, and brainstorm together. It also creates a valuable way to provide a mentoring relationship for students. There can even be specific purposes for creating a PLN such as this. Some examples include:

- Create a school safety committee or a health and wellness committee.
- Provide a tutoring program after school.
- Start a school spirit committee.

Sitting down with students and teachers together, learning to interact more beyond the classroom instruction, goes a long way to fostering relationships and setting a foundational structure for the school climate and a positive classroom culture.

3) Student-Led PD for PLP: In our classrooms, students are not the only learners, and teachers are not the only leaders. Together we share these roles. In schools today, we have to move past the perception that only the designated teacher can deliver the content. Students have the knowledge to share and will benefit from the chance to teach others. Learning becomes more powerful when we can draw on the talents of our students and colleagues and create more authentic and meaningful learning experiences for everyone. During most days of professional development, teachers often spend time in sessions on varying topics, possibly active with different tasks for the session or collaborating with peers. However, not every teacher enjoys this type of learning, and similar to the learning we want for our students, it needs to be more personal and fueled by choice.

Imagine inviting a few students to present during a professional development session. How inspiring it would be to learn from our students! Give them time to share some of their projects, offer student-approved tips about tools they enjoy using in class, or talk about the learning strategies that have helped them the most. When teachers can hear directly from the students and can then work with the students one-on-one, teacher-student relationships are fostered, and a bond that promotes the supportive networks that we need in our schools and in life is created. Think about some of the work your own students do in your class that may apply to other courses, or even innovative ideas they created on their own. These are the types of interactions that we want to promote. We must encourage students to share their work with a public audience (teachers and peers) and use this as a way to continue building relationships and showing students that their work has meaning and value.

4) Reverse Mentoring: In the movie *Men in Black*, "Agent J," new to the team, is paired with "Agent K," an experienced agent who is assigned to act as the mentor to J. Initially Agent K is irritated by the behaviors of Agent J, but as the movie progresses, we see a change in relationship and a dual mentorship is forming. A bit different from the way that mentorships typically work. They both had something to teach

and something to learn, although both kind of thought that they knew it all. Both had areas of professional and personal strengths and weaknesses, but they balanced each other well. Slightly different than the typical mentoring program, it showed the impact on professional practice regardless of your experience. As new teachers enter the profession and find their first teaching position, there likely is a program in the school for mentoring as part of a new teacher induction program. Typically, a veteran teacher is paired with a new teacher, whether first time teaching or new to the school. Depending on the experience in teacher preparation programs and how differently they can be set up, they may be very different from the preparation you had when you were a student. Hopefully, you had a positive experience, felt confident after completing your student teaching experience, and were ready to take on your own classroom, full of ideas, strategies, tools, and everything you needed to get started. If this was not your experience, or you graduated many years ago, before all of the digital tools, new ideas, trends and challenges in education came to be, you might find yourself feeling a bit out of the loop when it comes to the "talk" in education today. Typically in our schools, newer teachers are paired with a mentor to help them become accustomed to the school procedures and to feel comfortable in making the transition to a new school and possibly the first year of teaching. That's the conventional way of setting up a mentor program.

BUT INSTEAD, why not do something a little unconventional and give the idea of "reverse mentoring" a try. Reverse mentoring would involve setting up a connection different from the typical mentor/mentee partnerships. There would be a pairing between more veteran teachers with those newer to the teaching profession and/or new to the school. Or another possibility would be pairing up teachers who either teach completely different styles or content or grade levels, or who have a common interest in a teaching method, but are on different levels of comfort with it. Regardless of how the pairing is formed, there will not be a specified "mentor" or "mentee" in this collaboration. Both teachers will be part of the "mentorship," which can be used as a way to bridge any gaps when it comes to pedagogical knowledge, technological knowledge, and possibly content knowledge.

The idea behind reverse mentoring is that each teacher will have a colleague to work with and will be paired up based on factors such as strengths, areas of weakness, experience, content, or grade levels. There can even be colleagues paired up based on a common interest in something like blended learning, creating assessments, standards-based grading, or any relevant topic of interest.

The goal for the mentorship is to share knowledge of conventional methods and procedures while also exploring new, emerging ideas and trends to create more relevant and authentic learning experiences for students as well as for professional development. The teachers in the "mentorship" will balance each other and work collaboratively to grow their professional skills. Having these connections will be a positive way to build networks and foster cross-curricular collaborations to enhance student learning opportunities also.

Sometimes it is difficult to find time to work with peers and especially to stay current with all of the new trends and initiatives that happen in education. Changes come every day, and it can be overwhelming trying to figure out where to start, regardless of your years of experience. Often the more veteran teachers do not have enough time to explore digital tools for teaching concepts and can benefit from working with newer teachers who have recently gone through a teacher prep program or have perspectives from different schools that they can bring into the conversation. The newer teachers often have many responsibilities and things to remember when they are getting started, that it can be tough to balance the time to explore new ideas.

When experienced teachers have the opportunity to learn about new methods and tools, and at the same time, provide guidance for the newer teachers, it is mutually beneficial for them and their practice.

Just as with students in our classrooms, we work on helping them to build their network and peer collaborations, it is vitally important for educators to do the same thing.

To get started:

Step 1: Hold a meeting with all faculty members.

Step 2: Come up with topics/tools that faculty should know and implement.

Step 3: Ask faculty to find a partner for the mentorship.

Step 4: Make a list of five goals to work on. Some examples: tools for organization, assessment strategies and tools, blended learning, social-emotional learning, continued professional learning, or related topics focused on building the teaching practice and student success.

Step 5: Ask mentor teams to set a plan for meeting and follow-ups.

Step 6: Wrap it up by asking faculty members to share their plans.

AFTER A PERIOD OF A FEW WEEKS, it might be a good idea to bring everyone together to talk about what they have worked on and any benefits they have seen. Encourage everyone to provide honest feedback, look for the positives, and invite stories to be shared. Make time to address the negatives by asking about the drawbacks, the challenges, and be open to the conversation so that together you can revise the plan, adjust, and keep on going. Programs like this may take time at first, but hopefully, the impact is that other mentor teams may decide to join together and begin forming a PLN! It's about taking that first step and then making time to reflect and adjust along the way.

A learning family

We spend so much time within our classrooms and our school that we want to create a welcoming and supportive space for what ultimately becomes our learning family. It's so important to find ways to provide support for others but equally as important to find support for ourselves. Teaching can be an isolating profession if we let it. Because we are fully invested in doing what's best for students, being present in every moment, and providing for students in and out of the classroom, it can leave little time for our own needs. Our students have individual needs that we may not be aware of, and without adding in time or methods for students to connect with us more, we might miss opportunities to support them when they need it most. We must invest in ourselves so we can be the best for our students. We start by connecting and modeling the importance of becoming part of a larger learning community for our students.

Choose one of these ways to start building that PLN for you and your students. The best part about being in a PLN is that there is always room to learn and grow together, and to keep adding to the learning family. We do better when we connect with others and develop more awareness of the needs and experiences of those we lead and those we learn with. Start connecting today and see how quickly you have a new outlook on teaching and feel that support. Remember that you might not be able to meet in the same physical space, face-to-face, but the power of technology makes it possible to learn together in the virtual space and build powerful connections for learning.

Reflect

Think about your teaching experience before you started to become more connected. What did you do when you had questions about your practice or even frustrations that had built up? Who did you turn to for ideas or support? Or did you keep it to yourself, afraid to share your struggles with others? If you kept it to yourself, then it is time to act and build your network. Break away from the isolation and become connected. Choose one of these PLN Powerups and give it a try. Invite students to join in your conversations or to create their own PLN and work together. Reflect on these questions:

1. How does it benefit students when we are connected and part of a PLN?
2. Why is it important to involve students in our decisions and give them opportunities to lead?
3. What are some areas of teaching that you feel confident in? And what are some areas in which you could use a refresher?

These questions will guide you to decide which of these PLN Power building ideas will work best.

Begin connecting and learning on the go!

Start by connecting on Twitter if you are not already using it for learning. Start slow and see how it goes. Set aside time to get involved with a nightly chat. Here are a few that I participate in during the week and recommend:

Monday: #rethink_learning, #formativechat, #edtechchat, #learnlap, #tlap

Tuesday: #tnedchat, #PLN365, #stucentclass

Wednesday: #betheone, #ARVRinEDU

Thursday: #masterychat, #games4ed, #ditchbook

Friday: #engagechat

Saturday: #leadlap, #EduGladiators

Sunday: #bookcamppd

Action Steps

- Put yourself out there, ask questions, share your experience, and build new networks for you and your students. It just takes a few minutes to take that first step, and you will see how quickly your network forms and the benefits of being a connected educator.
- Look for a mentor within your school, perhaps even working with a student to exchange ideas about class activities, teaching strategies, and finding out how students learn best. When you are intentional about wanting to understand and meet the needs of students, your professional practice will be positively impacted.
- Choose one of the chats and just read through it for a few quick ideas!

#THRIVEinEDU

Once you get started with one of these ideas, share out with others by posting positive changes that have happened or what you've learned from pairing up in a reverse mentorship. Share to the hashtag #THRIVEinEDU.

10 FINAL THOUGHTS

There are so many ways that we can create uncommon, unique, student-driven learning experiences in our classrooms. As a teacher with almost 25 years of teaching experience, I wish I had more confidence or tried new things when I first started, or at least sometime during my first couple of years of teaching. I was too afraid to break away from the traditional methods, to get away from assigning homework, creating projects, giving tests, and being the only person talking in the classroom. I used my own experience as a student to guide my practice as a teacher. I tried everything that worked for me with my own students and stayed away from the methods and strategies that did not have an impact on me. But instead, what I should have done, what I could have done better was to allow students to share their thoughts with me.

We do have a responsibility to manage our classes and provide the right instruction and support for our students. We must make decisions based on what we hope will enable students to be successful in the future, whatever it is that they may ultimately decide to do. However, we can no longer hold the belief that we are the keepers of knowledge, that we are the only ones who can drive the instruction in the classroom. We have to be comfortable with making ourselves uncomfortable. What I mean is that we have to take some risks, put ourselves out there, and do things differently than we may have ever done before—to think differently and to involve students in the process of deciding what learning could and should look like in our classroom space.

Worried about making a mistake? Don't be. Our biggest mistake is in not taking action and keeping things the same. We have to try our own ideas and decide for ourselves what worked and what did not work, and why. And more importantly, involve our students in the discussion too. We then use this to continue our own professional growth as a way to stay current in our practice.

But it is uncomfortable...

We can do so much more for our students if we are intentional about breaking away from any isolation that we may have placed ourselves in, and instead disrupt our thinking. Push back against the mindset that we have to do things the way that they were done for us as students in the classroom, and remember that students have just as much to teach as they do to learn. We all have room to learn. Just take that step away from the comfortable place you've been and see what happens.

---

*"The comfort zone is the great enemy to **creativity**; moving beyond it necessitates intuition, which in turn configures new perspectives and conquers fears."*

DAN STEVENS

Start Somewhere

It can feel overwhelming to try new things in the classroom, but remember that you only have to start with one thing. There are so many great ideas, strategies, and new tools that educators may feel lost as to where or how to begin. You don't have to do it all. Instead, choose one of the many ideas from this book and give it a go. A good friend of mine, Jaime Donally, offered great advice while we were presenting on the topic of AR and VR. Some attendees were concerned with knowing how to get started with these new tools in their classrooms. Jaime responded by saying, "Plus One." She said, just start with one thing and work with it. When you feel ready, add something else. One thing at a time, moving forward and learning with students.

We are all learning as we go. We have to take those risks in our class-rooms and put ourselves out there so that our students will become more confident and comfortable taking risks too. We learn just as much, if not more, from failures as we do from successes. There is always room to improve, and we owe it to our students and ourselves to break away from what we have been doing. Try something different, unique, and unconventional.

Reflect

1. Look around your classroom—what does the learning space look like? What are some ways that you can make a change today?
2. Think about the amount of time you get to interact with your students and how much they get to interact with one another. How can you change that for them and for you?
3. Consider how you spend your time when you are not teaching. Are you making time to connect, or staying in your

own space? How can you create opportunities to work with your peers more often?

#THRIVEinEDU

Think about the new ideas you learned from reading this book. Try something and share it with others. Make time to share your story, your successes, and failures, and use these to guide your next steps and to create new opportunities for your students. Share out with others by posting some of the positive changes you have experienced, or the risks you took and the failures that helped you to grow. As educators, we know that learning still happens, even in failure. Rather than focusing on goals that we did not reach yet or mistakes that we made along the way, ask yourself one question that Daniel Pink, author of *Drive*, asked: "Was I a little better today than yesterday?" (Pink, 2009, p. 136).

That is all it takes. Think about the progress that you make each day and use your experiences to help students face their own challenges. Inspire others to act and to continue to grow by sharing your story to the hashtag #THRIVEinEDU.

QUICKSTART ESSENTIALS

1. **Relationships**: Don't just learn their name, know who they are. It is important to spend time throughout the year getting to really know students. Use icebreakers, games, and activities to build relationships and student PLN. We need to build those vital connections within our classrooms.

2. **More than one leader**: Teachers are not the only leaders in the classroom. It's time to move away from thinking there must be a lead learner. Put students in the lead more. How about trying "Teacher for a Day," and let them lead, have students create lessons to teach peers and see them become more empowered and confident in the classroom. Create a class review collaborative presentation, and think differently about "review sessions."

3. **Homework and assessments**: We do not always have to create everything for our students. Why not try Choose Your Own Assessments and have students create and provide multiple ways to promote student-driven learning, inquiry, and personalization. Don't give homework just to give homework, and especially not simply worksheets, or

outlining, watching videos that are the same for all students. Why give homework at all? Let's open up choices and opportunities for active and meaningful learning, not compliance.

4. **Show what you know:** Let students decide how to practice, explore and build their skills, become self-aware, and find their interests. What are some other ways to assess students... why does it have to be a test?

5. **Points and grades**: How often we are asked, "Am I getting points for this? Is this for a grade?" Let's work to help students move away from focusing on the point value and instead focus more on the value in the process of learning. Let's foster that growth mindset.

6. **Grading policies:** Let's rethink the way we grade and how we deduct points and strive to understand why students are turning in work late. Are they still mastering the content but lacking in organizational skills? Do something different, be open to adapting based on each student, have open conversations, and clear expectations.

7. **Projects and presentations**: Break the traditional pattern of having every student do their own project where only the teacher sees it. Why not have the class do collaborative presentations, sharing as they work, building more than just content skills. Use these opportunities to work on SEL, collaboration and communication, vital skills, and competencies that our students need.

8. **Projects that are over and done:** Give them a new purpose! Take what the students create and use their projects for enrichment /extended activities, instructional materials for years to come. Build a learner-driven classroom, creating and sharing authentic work, helping them to feel the value of contributing and being teachers /leaders themselves.

9. **Routines, rules, and procedures:** Get students more involved in classroom design and practices. Establish classroom

practices as a group, let the students create their way to practice for the class period.

10. **Technology**: Even if you don't teach a technology course, we need to prepare our students for the future. Find ways to enhance what you are doing by adding in a little bit of tech. Let students decide what to use and take more ownership in learning.

11. **Classroom structure and movement:** In the classroom, no more sit and get for our students—let's make the most out of our class time. Encourage students to create and design class time. Create a space for students to design, to display their work, their quotes, and make it their own.

12. **Everything by the book**! How about we forget about the book and create our own materials? Don't be "bound" by the book and its content. Be real and authentic.

13. **Unreal experiences:** Augmented and virtual reality can be used in any class. Take students on a learning adventure around the world, right from within your classroom space.

14. **Feedback**: Conversations with students and checking in daily and weekly are important. How can you build time into your classroom for those critical conversations? Use Genius Hour, 20% time, choose your own/choice boards, stations.

15. **Parent communication:** Engage parents more in what is happening in the classroom. Learn about family access to technology and set up innovative ways to share information through messaging tools, class webpage, blogs, student video responses, podcasts, and more. Bring the classroom happenings to the family. http://bit.ly/parentfive

These may be somewhat "unconventional" shifts, but they will offer different ideas and strategies that perhaps will lead to unbelievable learning experiences for students.

If you feel like you're too different or your ideas are too strange because you may be the only one doing them, that is perfectly fine! Dare to be different and have students experience different! We need to spark student curiosity for learning. By extending our own learning and taking our own risks, we will foster a love of lifelong learning.

SUGGESTED RESOURCES: A FEW OF MY FAVORITES FOR GATHERING IDEAS

Blogs

- DefinedSTEM
- EdSurge
- Getting Smart
- Teach Thought
- Learning as I go

Podcasts

- Andrew Wheelock (Coffee with a Geek)
- Barbara Bray (Rethink Learning)
- Brad Shreffler (Planning Period Podcast)
- Dan Kreiness (Leader of Learning)
- Dave Schmittou (Lasting Learning)
- Denis Sheeran (Instant Relevance Podcast)
- Don Wettrick (StartEDUp)
- EduMatch Tweet and Talk

- Glen Irvin and Mike Washburn (OnEducation Podcast)
- Jennifer Gonzalez (Cult of Pedagogy)
- Teach Better Team Podcast
- Vicki Davis (Ten Minute Teacher)
- Will Deyamport (The Dr. Will Show, The Edupreneur)
- Weston Kieschnick (Teaching Keating)

Twitter Hashtags

- #ARVRinEDU
- #BetheOne
- #BookcampPD
- #EduGladiators
- #EduMatch
- #Edtechchat
- #Engagechat
- #FormativeChat
- #LearnLAP
- #Masterychat
- #PD4uandMe
- #PLN365
- #Rethink_Learning
- #teachbetter
- #teachpos
- #TLAP

REFERENCES

Boss, S., & Larmer, J. (2018). Project-based teaching: How to create rigorous and engaging learning experiences. Alexandria, VA: ASCD.

Burgess, D. (2012). *Teach like a pirate*. San Diego, CA: DAVE BURGESS CONSULTING.

Cooper, R., & Murphy, E. (2017). *Hacking project-based learning: 10 easy steps to PBL and inquiry in the classroom*. TIMES 10 PUBLICATIONS.

Donally, J. (2018). Learning transported: Augmented, virtual, and mixed reality for all classrooms. Portland, OR: International Society for Technology in Education.

Ertmer, P. (1999). Addressing first- and second-order barriers to change: strategies for technology integration. Educational Technology Research and Development, 47(4), 47-61. Retrieved from http://www.jstor.org/stable/30221096

Highfill, L., Hilton, K., & Landis, S. (2016). The HyperDoc handbook: Digital lesson design using Google apps. Irvine, CA: EdTechTeam Press.

Pink, D. H. (2009). *Drive: The surprising truth about what motivates us*. New York, NY: Riverhead Books.

Rogers, E. (2003). Diffusion of innovations: 5th ed. New York: Free Press.

Sheninger, E. C., & Murray, T. C. (2017). Learning transformed: 8 keys to designing tomorrow's schools, today. Alexandria, VA: ASCD. page 115

The 5 Stages of Technology Adoption. (2012). Retrieved May 16, 2019, from https://ondigitalmarketing.com/learn/odm/foundations/5-customer-segments-technology-adoption/

Thomas, S., Howard, N. R., & Schaffer, R. (2019). Closing the gap: Digital equity strategies for the K-12 classroom. Portland, OR: International Society for Technology in Education.

Tucker, C. R., Wycoff, T., & Green, J. T. (2017). Blended learning in action: A practical guide toward sustainable change. Thousand Oaks, CA: Corwin, a SAGE company.

Webb, N. L. (2002). Depth of knowledge for mathematics, science, technology, & mathematics (STEM). Retrieved on July 25, 2019. doi:10.4135/9781483377544.n6

Wettrick, D. (2017). Pure genius. (2017). San Diego, CA: Dave Burgess Consulting.

Movies and TV Programs Referenced

Herek, S. (Director). (1989). Bill & Ted's excellent adventure [Motion picture]. United States, MGM Studios

Hughes, J. D. (Director). (1986). Ferris Bueller's day off [Motion picture]. United States. Paramount Pictures.

LaGravenese, R. (Director). (2007). Freedom writers [Motion picture]. United States: Paramount home entertainment.

Linklater, R. (Director). (2003). School of rock [Motion picture]. United States. Paramount Studios.

Menendez, R., Musca, T., Olmos, E. J., Phillips, L. D., De, S. R., Garcia, A., & Safan, C., ... Warner Home Video (1988). Stand and deliver. [Motion picture]. United States. American Playhouse.

Weir, Peter. (Director). (1989). Dead poet's society
[Motion picture]. United States: Buena Vista
Pictures Distribution.

Welcome back Kotter [Television series]. (n.d.).

ABOUT THE AUTHOR

Rachelle Dene Poth is a longtime French, Spanish, and STEAM Teacher, and an EdTech Consultant, the Founder of THRIVEinEDU LLC. She is also an attorney and has a Master's Degree in Instructional Technology. Rachelle serves as President of the ISTE Teacher Education Network and is on the Leadership Team for the Mobile Learning Network. She received the Making IT Happen Award at ISTE 2019 and a Presidential Gold Award for Volunteer Service to Education in 2018 and 2019. She was selected as one of "20 to watch" by the NSBA and the PAECT Outstanding Teacher of the Year in 2017. Rachelle is a Future Ready Instructional Coach. She is an

EduGladiator Core Warrior and an Affiliate of the Pushing Boundaries Consulting LLC. Rachelle is a Buncee Ambassador, Edmodo Certified Trainer, and Nearpod PioNear.

Rachelle is the author of *In Other Words: Quotes That Push Our Thinking*, *The Future is Now: Looking Back to Move Ahead* (EduGladiators), and *Chart a New Course: A Guide to Teaching Essential Skills for Tomorrow's World* (ISTE, March 2020.) Rachelle has two additional books due in 2020. She is a contributing author to several books, including *Education Write Now* Volume 3 (December 2019), *EduMatch Snapshot in Education* 2016, 2017, 2018, and 2019, *Gamify Literacy*, an ISTE publication, and *Stories in EDU*. She is a blogger for DefinedSTEM, NEO LMS, and Getting Smart. She is the host of #Formativechat on Mondays and maintains her "Learning as I Go" blog site at http://www.Rdene915.com. Check out her podcast on Anchor. Connect with Rachelle on Twitter @Rdene915.

OTHER EDUMATCH TITLES

In Other Words by Rachelle Dene Poth
In Other Words is a book full of inspirational and thought-provoking quotes that have pushed the author's thinking and inspired her.

EduMatch Snapshot in Education (2016)
In this collaborative project, twenty educators located throughout the United States share educational strategies that have worked well for them, both with students and in their professional practice.

The #EduMatch Teacher's Recipe Guide
Editors: Tammy Neil & Sarah Thomas
Dive in as fourteen international educators share their recipes for success, both literally and metaphorically!

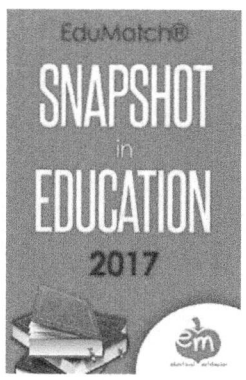

EduMatch Snapshot in Education (2017)
We're back! EduMatch proudly presents Snapshot in Education (2017). In this two-volume collection, 32 educators and one student share their tips for the classroom and professional practice.

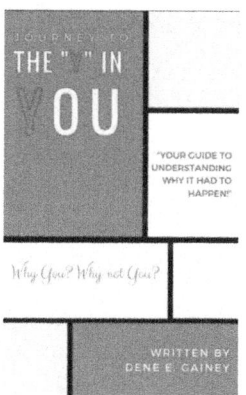

Journey to The "Y" in You by Dene Gainey
This book started as a series of separate writing pieces that were eventually woven together to form a fabric called The Y in You. The question is, "What's the 'why' in you?"

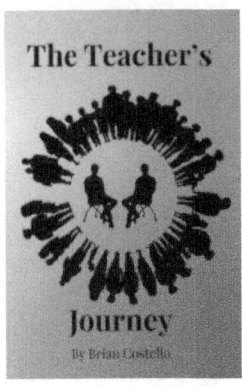

The Teacher's Journey by Brian Costello
Follow the Teacher's Journey with Brian as he weaves together the stories of seven incredible educators. Each step encourages educators at any level to reflect, grow, and connect.

The Fire Within
Compiled and edited by Mandy Froehlich
Adversity itself is not what defines us. It is how we react to that adversity and the choices we make that creates who we are and how we will persevere.

EduMagic by Sam Fecich
This book challenges the thought that "teaching" begins only after certification and college graduation. Instead, it describes how students in teacher preparation programs have value to offer their future colleagues, even as they are learning to be teachers!

Makers in Schools
Editors: Susan Brown & Barbara Liedahl
The maker mindset sets the stage for the Fourth Industrial Revolution, empowering educators to guide their students.

Divergent EDU by Mandy Froehlich
The concept of being innovative can be made to sound so simple. But what if the development of the innovative thinking isn't the only roadblock?

EduMatch Snapshot in Education (2018)
EduMatch® is back for our third annual Snapshot in Education. Dive in as 21 educators share a snapshot of what they learned, what they did, and how they grew in 2018.

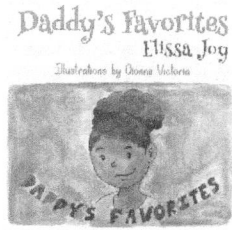

Daddy's Favorites by Elissa Joy
Illustrated by Dionne Victoria
Five-year-old Jill wants to be the center of everyone's world. But, her most favorite person in the world, without fail, is her Daddy. But Daddy has to be Daddy, and most times that means he has to be there when everyone needs him, especially when her brother Danny needs him.

Level Up Leadership by Brian Kulak
Gaming has captivated its players for generations and cemented itself as a fundamental part of our culture. In order to reach the end of the game, they all need to level up.

DigCit Kids edited by Marialice Curran & Curran Dee

This book is a compilation of stories, starting with our own mother and son story, and shares examples from both parents and educators on how they embed digital citizenship at home and in the classroom. (Also available in Spanish)

Stories of EduInfluence by Brent Coley

In Stories of EduInfluence, veteran educator Brent Coley shares stories from more than two decades in the classroom and front office.

The Edupreneur by Dr. Will

The Edupreneur is a 2019 documentary film that takes you on a journey into the successes and challenges of some of the most recognized names in K-12 education consulting.

To Whom it May Concern

Editors: Sarah-Jane Thomas, PhD & Nicol R. Howard, PhD

In To Whom it May Concern..., you will read a collaboration between two Master's in Education classes at two universities on opposite coasts of the United States.

One Drop of Kindness by Jeff Kubiak
This children's book, along with each of you, will change our world as we know it. It only takes One Drop of Kindness to fill a heart with love.

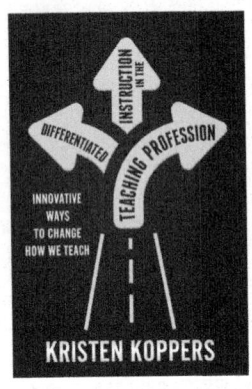

DI in the Teaching Profession by Kristen Koppers
Differentiated Instruction in the Teaching Profession is an innovative way to use critical thinking skills to create strategies to help all students succeed.

L.E.A.D. from Day One by Ryan McHale
L.E.A.D. from Day One is a go-to resource to help educators outline a future plan toward becoming a teacher leader.

Unlock Creativity by Jacie Maslyk
Every classroom is filled with creative potential. Unlock Creativity will help you discover opportunities that will make every student see themselves as a creative thinker.

Make Waves! by Hal Roberts

In Make Waves! Hal discusses 15 attributes of a great leader. He shares his varied experience as a teacher, leader, a player in the N.F.L., and a plethora of research to take you on a journey to emerge as leader of significance.

21 Lessons of Tech Integration Coaching by Martine Brown

In 21 Lessons of Tech Integration Coaching, Martine Brown provides a practical guide about how to use your skills to support and transform schools.

Cover images drawn by Hann Morrissey, grade 10. Hann designed the cover for my first book, In Other Words. The trees are a mix of new designs and pieces of the original cover, representing the importance of trying new things, pushing for growth, and connecting so together we can thrive.

Made in the USA
Monee, IL
25 February 2020